WOMEN IN GOLF

THE PLAYERS, THE HISTORY, AND THE FUTURE OF THE SPORT

DAVID L. HUDSON, JR.

Westport, Connecticut
London

Library of Congress Cataloging-in-Publication Data

Hudson, David L., 1969–
    Women in golf : the players, the history, and the future of the sport / David L. Hudson, Jr.
        p. cm.
    Includes bibliographical references and index.
    ISBN 978–0–275–99784–7 (alk. paper)
    1. Golf for women—United States. 2. Women golfers—United States—Biography 3. Sex
discrimination in sports—United States. 4. Ladies Professional Golf Association. I. Title.
GV966.H83 2008
796.3520922—dc22   2007030424
[B]

British Library Cataloguing in Publication Data is available.

Library of Congress Catalog Card Number: 2007030424
ISBN: 978–0–275–99784–7

First published in 2008

Praeger Publishers, 88 Post Road West, Westport, CT 06881
An imprint of Greenwood Publishing Group, Inc.
www.praeger.com

Printed in the United States of America

The paper used in this book complies with the
Permanent Paper Standard issued by the National
Information Standards Organization (Z39.48-1984).

10 9 8 7 6 5 4 3 2 1

To the memory of my beloved grandmother,
Rose Kostadin Krusa,
who loved the great game of golf
with all of her beautiful soul and spirit.

CONTENTS

ACKNOWLEDGMENTS

I would like to thank everyone at Greenwood Press who helped make this book a reality, as well as those at BeaconPMG who put it to final print. I appreciate all of your hard work. I would like to thank the following people who provided expert comments, suggestions, ideas, or other information: Rhonda Glenn of the USGA, surely one of the finest writers on golf and former great amateur player herself; Eric Fleming, whose passion for Se Ri Pak and other Korean women golfers is inspiring; Pam Swensen, who battles for women in golf and business regularly at the Executive Women's Golf Association; professor and author Susan E. Cayleff for her insights on the great Babe and for her excellent writing on that legendary performer; Janet Coles, former LPGA professional winner and teacher of golf, for her insights on the tour and the game; friends Doris and David Kim for their insights on Korean culture; Tennessean editorial writer Dwight Lewis, for his comments on race and sports; expert attorney Marsha Kazarosian, for her legal advocacy on behalf of those who face discrimination on golf courses because of gender; professor of sociology and sports Dana Brooks for his insights on race in sport and Althea Gibson; golf historian extraordinaire Jim Healey for his wisdom and advice; and the gracious and great Charlie Mechem, former LPGA commissioner who provided many keen insights about the Tour. I would also like to thank the following individuals whose work served as invaluable sources for this project: Basil Ashton Tinkler, Liz Kahn, Rhonda Glenn, Elinor Nickerson, Clifton Brown, and Mark Frost, among others. Most of all I would like to thank my loving parents for the educational opportunities they provided and my wife Carla for her unwavering support and love.

CHAPTER 1

GOLF'S ORIGINS

It has been truthfully said that of all games, golf is the most beneficial and enjoyable for women.

—F. W. Crane[1]

Women can play golf and play it well. It does not impose any tax upon their systems, but provides them with a simple, healthful, open-air exercise.

—The *New York Times*[2]

It is, moreover, a picturesque game, and here it appeals to women, who have fallen victimization to its fascinations by the thousands.

—F. Johnston Roberts[3]

"It consists of putting little balls into little holes with instruments very ill adapted to this purpose."[4] This popular adage beautifully describes the game of golf, a maddeningly frustrating but eminently rewarding game that is played by millions all over the world. Given the obsessive natures of many of its ardent admirers, one might think that the origins of golf would be settled historical fact. Such is not the case, as the origins of golf remain a mystery disputed by historians from different countries. The *Chicago Tribune* in 1892 reported that "the origin of golf is hazy and uncertain."[5] Some say it comes from ancient Rome. Others say it comes from Japan, France, the Netherlands, China, or Scotland. "Like some complex jigsaw puzzle with many of the key pieces missing, its early history remains vague and incomplete," writes Dale Concannon in his *Golf: The Early Days.*[6]

In Rome, soldiers often played a game called *paganica,* which involved hitting a leather ball with a bent stick. Others point to the English game cambucca, or cambuc. This game involved a wooden ball hit with a curved club. King Edward III issued a proclamation in 1363 ordering "able-bodied men" on their days of rest to play sport with their bows and arrows and forbade "football" and "cambuc." The French played a game called *jeu de mail*, which involved a wooden ball hit down "fairways." Called pall mall in England, some historians claim it to be a progenitor of modern golf. Still others point to the Dutch game of *spel metten kolve*, or *kolf*. Traced back to 1297, the game involved hitting a ball over long distances, often icy canals, on 4-hole courses.[7]

Many historians claim the sport originated in Scotland, where many members of the royal family played the game regularly. The game spread rapidly in Scotland to the extent that several monarchs through the years issued bans on golf for fear that it would undermine the country's defenses because soldiers were playing golf instead of patrolling and providing protection.[8]

King James II banned golf in 1457 when he thought that his subjects were foregoing their archery practice in favor of idly playing golf or football. His edict proclaimed: "futebaw and golf be utterly cryt done and not usyt."[9] The royal edict ordered the men to practice on archery ranges. Instead, many ignored the edict and continued their obsession with golf—an addiction with which many in the twenty-first century can likely empathize.

The game was played by royalty and common folk on an increasing number of courses. Golf courses were built in Edinburgh, St. Andrews, Perth, Montrose, Leven, Dornoch, Banff, and Aberdeen.

King James IV of Scotland played golf even though he had issued an edict in 1491 banning the practice. Allegedly, some barons convinced James to give the game a try. Finally, the king relented and took a few swings in 1502. He could not believe his ineptness at this "ridiculous sport" but kept trying to improve his swing. Concannon writes: "Soon he was hooked—the golfing bug had bitten him and James IV became an enthusiastic convert."[10]

James IV bought golfing clothes and spent an entire February one year playing the game and hunting. He introduced the game to England on his visits to the royal court of Henry VIII. One of Henry VIII's wives, Catherine of Aragon, apparently had some connection to the game. She wrote: "I shall not so often hear from the King....I thank God I am busy with the golfe."[11] Unfortunately for her, Catherine could not give Henry a child and she was discarded for another wife, Anne Boleyn.

Most historians recognize Mary, Queen of Scots, as the first woman to have played golf regularly. She played both golf and pall mall. One historian writes that "she even played golf on the links close to the Fifth of Forth."[12] Another writes that "she played at golf and pall-mall."[13] A mysterious and tragic historical figure, Mary lost her life in part to her love of golf.

Mary learned the game at an early age and played it after she was moved to France as a young girl to marry the French Dauphin, Francois, at the age of fifteen. While in France, Mary played the game regularly with French students called cadets who were forced to carry her clubs. This led to the term caddy. After the Dauphin died, Mary returned to Scotland. As she was the rightful heir to the throne of England, she was considered a threat to her cousin, Queen Elizabeth of England.

Mary married Lord Darnley, who later was murdered. Some speculated for years that Mary was involved in the murder of her husband. Years later, her cousin, the Earl of Moray, testified against her, saying that she had played golf only a few days after Lord Darnley's death. Historian Alison Weir writes: "Mary's enemies were later to make up all kinds of scurrilous tales about her visit to Seton...[including] playing golf and pall-mall."[14]

Nearly all accounts of golf history deal with men, not women. Elinor Nickerson notes in her book *Golf: A Women's History:* "All during the time from the days of Mary, Queen of Scots, to the close of the eighteenth century, a period of more than 200 years, women are not mentioned in connection with the history of the game of golf. The usual accounts of the development of golf make it appear as though no female ever placed a hand on a golf club to take a swing at a golf ball."[15] However, women have loved the game of golf as much as, if not more than, men have. One American newspaper reported near the end of the nineteenth century: "Golfing women are said to be more enthusiastic over their favorite game than half the men who play on the 'links.'"[16]

Scottish fishwives played golf at Musselburgh in 1810 in a tournament for a first prize of "creel and a skull"—a fish basket with handkerchiefs.[17] The women received a tournament only after they pointed out that the men had one and they did not. Nickerson reports that some women golfers were responsible in 1842 for a significant change to the official rules of golf—that a golfer could lift and drop a ball without penalty when it was not playable. She notes that "surely it is reasonable to assume that women's interest in the game and in this particular rule sprang from something more than mere spectator participation."[18]

British women formed their own golf clubs in the 1860s. The St. Andrews Ladies Golf Club formed in 1867, and other clubs formed a few years later. As more and more women played, they desired more formal competition—a chance to test their skills against others. Enter Issette Pearson. Rhonda Glenn writes: "It was Miss Pearson's dedication that launched women's golf down an often treacherous path to the glory and riches that await today's best players."[19]

Pearson, an excellent player in her own right, organized a meeting at the Grand Hotel on London's Trafalgar Square in April 1893 of several different ladies' golf clubs. The result was the LGU (Ladies Golf Union), which eventually established the first national championship. In June 1893 the women held the first championship at the Royal Lytham and St. Anne's Golf Course.

LADY MARGARET SCOTT

The winner of the inaugural British championship was a young 18-year-old woman named Lady Margaret Scott. The daughter of John Scott, the third Earl of Eldon, or Lord Eldon, Margaret learned the game at a young age in Gloucester. Her father had "an almost perfect course" at Stowell Park.[20] She learned the game naturally, picking it up much better than her sister Louisa. Margaret was such a fine golfer that she had won a tournament at the Cheltenham club against men players.[21]

The tournament at Royal Lytham was played in a match-play format, which meant that players matched up one on one, advancing to successive rounds. In the final round Lady Margaret Scott faced Issette Pearson. Lady Margaret was simply too good for Pearson, winning by a score of 7 holes up with 5 to play, or 7 and 5. "Following Lady Margaret's win, her father made her victory speech for her," Glenn reports.[22] Lady Margaret won the next two British championships as well. In 1894, she faced Mrs. Ernest Catterall, an excellent player in her own right. Glenn reports that an unknown poet wrote the following poem about the encounter:

> E. Catterall would scatter all,
> If in the fateful draw
> She had not got the champion Scott
> Who is a gowfer braw.[23]

Lady Margaret won the match 6 and 5 to advance to the finals for a rematch against Pearson. This time Pearson played tougher, but Lady Margaret still prevailed by a score of 3 and 2.

In 1895, Lady Margaret made it a three-peat by winning the championship—this time held in Ireland—over Miss Emma Lythgoe 5 and 4. Truly, no one could stop the "gowfer braw." Lady Margaret never played another British championship. She married a Swiss gentleman and moved there. She won three Swiss Open championships as Lady Hamilton Russell.[24]

Some of the reported scores of Lady Margaret shooting in the 70s even with the more primitive equipment of those days compel the question of how she would compare to great golfers that came after her. Such comparisons are difficult, if not downright impossible. But there was no doubt that Lady Margaret was a superb golfer. Gillian Kirkwood, an executive council member of the LGU, says:

She could certainly hold her own in men's company, and in 1892 she won a championship at Cheltenham where the rest her opponents were men, and made the best scratch score, a 70 at Bath in similar company. There would be no Ladies tees in those days. Famous golfers such as Cecil Leitch, Joyce Wethered, Glenna Collett, Jessie Valentine, Babe Zaharias, right up to the present day with Annika Sorenstam have all played more and won more. Lady Margaret's era was very short-lived, and the events that she played in were very few. However when she did play, she won everything, and was only ever once down in a match...against Mrs Ryder-Richardson in the semi-final at Portrush in 1895, and even then she turned it around and won, and went on to win the British Championship for the third consecutive time.[25]

Kirkwood explains further:

In those early days of ladies' golf, most men really did not believe that golf was a game for women, and it was Lady Margaret Scott who changed their minds. Her youth, beauty, flawless swing and winning results caught the imagination of the time. Women realized that they could leave the putting greens, play golf on long courses and aspire to the high standards of Lady Margaret Scott. In those early days of ladies' golf, Lady Margaret Scott was truly a champion.[26]

The golf craze continued in Britain among both sexes, as the sport grew in popularity. One report referred to the "death of lawn tennis" in England because more and more people were turning to golf instead.[27]

GOLF IN AMERICA

Golf also took off in America—among both men and women. The *Washington Post* reported in 1890 that "some girls are anxious to learn golf, because they are really fond of sport and exercise; others, because it gives them a chance to show off a natty suit."[28] Early descriptions of the game focus more on the attire of female golfers than their actual prowess—or lack thereof—of the new game. Those in so-called high society found it fashionable to try their hand at this new and exciting game. The *New York Times* reported in 1891 that "an outdoor pastime which appears to be gaining favor in this country, and especially in the vicinity of New York, is the Scottish national game of golf."[29] Three golf clubs formed in New York—the Yonkers, the Meadowbrook, and the Shinnecock Hills Club. The reported members of the club were all males.[30] The *Chicago Tribune* reported the next year in 1892 that "golf is the coming game."[31] The paper noted that many young women had become "golf widows before their honeymoon was barely over" because of the addictiveness of this new sport or pastime.

The great English author and poet Rudyard Kipling introduced the game of golf in Vermont when he visited in 1893. "Mr. Kipling's introduction of the game into this country may possible induce some of our American writers, many of whom are fond of sports, to take it up," wrote one newspaper.[32] Baltimore College considered introducing the game to its young women as part of a new physical education program after one of its directors saw the popularity of many sports, including golf, among young English women students.[33]

It became apparent that women were not to be denied the ability to play golf. Their passion for the game was equal to that of men. The *New York Times* explained in 1894: "Golf is not limited to any particular class of individuals. Ladies and children can play the game as well as men, and in nearly all the golf clubs which have been recently organized the women show as keen an interest as the men themselves."[34]

In 1894, a group of women in Morristown, New Jersey, organized for themselves a golf club—the first of its kind in the United States. The *New York Times* reported that it is "the only golf club in this country that has been completely organized and brought to a point of assured success by ladies."[35] The women were the members of the so-called Morris County Golf Club and were the officers of the club, with the men serving in advisor capacity. "It is offered and run exclusively by the gentler sex, who have proven liberal, discreet and sportsmanlike in all of the rulings."[36] Only when a woman agreed to "put up" a man was he allowed to enjoy the privileges of the club.

In October 1894 eight women at the Morris County Golf Club competed in the first tournament for the grand prize of a $1,000 silver cup made by Tiffany & Co. The eight competitors played 7 holes. Miss Annie Howland Ford navigated the 7 holes with a score of 48 to capture the cup. The scores ranged from 48 to 72.[37] Probably the best player at the Morris Country Club was Mrs. William Shippen, who set a club record with a 78 over 18 holes in September 1897.

A few days later, fifteen women competed at the Morris County Golf Club over the 7-hole course. Miss Ford did not play this time but served as the official scorer. This time the winning score was turned in by Mrs. William Shippen, who carded a 54 to win by one stroke over Mrs. Arthur Dean and Miss Lois Raymond. It was Raymond who brought laughter to those in attendance when she "was moved to express her mind freely and firmly by ejaculating 'Isn't it mean' when the club which ought to have sent the ball far out into the field merely grazed the top, moving it but a few inches along the teeing ground."[38]

Women also began playing at Southampton, Long Island, and at the Meadow Brooks Country Club in New York. At Shinnecock, Long Island, women played in a handicap tournament in late October 1894. Miss Sarah Livingstone won the event.[39] In May 1895, it was announced that a women's club tournament would be held in Staten Island. The game became very popular among men and women in Newport, Rhode Island. The *New York Times* reported that "golf is becoming a universal sport here this season."[40] Mrs. W. Butler Duncan, Jr., won the President's Cup at the Newport links in an 1895 tournament with a 9-hole score of 67.[41]

Still the game was often dominated by those in high society. "Golf has not become a favorite in America and is still taken up more or less as a fad among the ultra-fashionable."[42]

Slowly, the game spread across the country. The *Los Angeles Times* even ran a piece in 1895 entitled "Athletic Grandmammas," telling readers that many a grandmother had taken to the golf links and other athletic ventures.[43]

The continued interest in the game among women caused the United States Golf Association to hold its first national tournament. In 1896, twenty-five women competed at the Morris County Golf Club in Morristown, New Jersey, for the coveted prize. While Mrs. Charles S. Brown had won a similar event at Meadowbrook, that event was "hastily arranged" and had "barely a dozen competitors."[44] The 1896 championship was "really the first tournament for ladies managed on a genuine championship level."[45]

Indeed, the sport had taken seize in America by 1896. In his piece "The Golf Season of 1896" F.W. Crane wrote for the *New York Times*:

The golf season which has just closed has been the most successful in more respects than one that America has ever seen. The growing popularity of the game would naturally lead to such a result, and it is not at all improbable that each succeeding year will exceed the other in the excellence of its golf and enthusiasm for the sport. In a wonderfully short space of time this ancient Scottish game has leaped into the front rank of America's outdoor achievements, and if any sport-loving individual still entertains doubt as to the solid hold already acquired by golf let him visit some of the clubs in the vicinity of New York on any legal holiday or Saturday afternoon and he will find the club course teeming with players, ladies enjoying the invigorating exercise as well men.[46]

— CHAPTER 2 —

EARLY GREATS OF THE GAME

In the early days, the best golfers came from Great Britain—England, Scotland, and Ireland. Golf first took off in this part of the world. The best men and women players came from these countries.

"It's similar to the development of men's golf in Great Britain as compared to the development of men's golf in the United States that a number of women in England, Ireland and Scotland began playing golf before it was popularized in the United States," says Rhonda Glenn.

The British Open Ladies Amateur, in fact, began in 1893, two years before the United States Golf Association conducted the U.S. Women's Amateur, the first national championship here for women. Women in Great Britain also founded the Ladies Golf Union, the governing body for women's golf in that country, shortly before the 1893 British Ladies Open Amateur. This ruling body, although it first had men as officers, fostered women's golf in that country and has conducted the British Ladies Open Amateur ever since.[1]

While the best players still resided in England and Scotland, Americans took to golf like fish to water. British champion Henry James Whigham ventured across the Atlantic Ocean in 1895 to observe America and its growing obsession with golf. He commented:

There is no question that the growth of golf here has been much more rapid than during a similar space of time in England, and some of the best players who have learned the game on their home links within the past three years have attained an excellent degree of perfection.... The American golfers take hold of the game with an energy and enthusiasm not noticeable on the other side, and quickly attain an able game, if not in all respects a finished game.[2]

However, Whigham quickly added that the best players in the world resided in England and Scotland, noting that "they have been at it longer." Still, the surge of British pride shone through the gentleman's comments as he added: "America has yet no golfers who could be compared favorably with the first-rate golfers in Great Britain."[3]

Yet, golf continued to grow in popularity in America. The *Washington Post* had reported as early as 1893 that golf had become a "popular fad," particularly among "Washington society." The newspaper described the game and its appeal: "The players become very expert in lifting and driving the ball with the golf sticks, and as it is like tennis in that it can be varied from the lightest recreation to downright hard work. It is popular with all ages and sexes."[4]

The paper added that the game "is popular with all ages and sexes."[5] In 1897, the *Chicago Daily Tribune* ran a piece that said women players "are running the men a close second in the contest for honors in the game."[6]

In 1905, the stage was set for a historic clash between American female golfers and their counterparts from the British Isles. The Executive Committee of the Ladies' Golf Union set the match in London between British and American women. The British women dominated 6 to 1. The lone bright spot for the Americans was Miss Georgianna Bishop of Bridgeport, Connecticut, who defeated tennis champion and English golf champion Lottie Dodd. According to newspaper accounts, "Miss May Hezlett, the Irish champion, outclassed Miss Margaret Curtis."[7]

"Great Britain—which includes Scotland, Ireland and Wales—had the best players, if you look at the number of good players, for many years," Glenn says. "It wasn't really until Alexa Stirling and Glenna Collett came along that America could boast of really great players, although the USA had fine ones. Collett, however, was unable to defeat the famed English player, Joyce Wethered, in their encounters in the British championship."[8]

RHONA ADAIR

Rhona Adair was a fine Irish golfer who won the championship of Great Britain in 1900 and 1903. In May 1903, she defeated Miss Florence Walker Leigh in Dublin, Ireland, at the Portrush Club by a score of 4 and 2. She could not retain her title in 1904, falling to May Hezlet in the fourth round 4 and 2.

MAY HEZLET

Arguably the finest golfer during the turn of the century was a young woman named Mary Linzee Hezlet—known as May. She learned the game at an early age with her sisters Florence and Violet, who also became accomplished players. Her mother Mrs. Hezlet played competitive golf too, playing in the British champions for more than 30 years, even as a 77-year-old in the 1924 tournament.

The best of the Hezlet family was May, who won five Irish Ladies Closed Championships in Ireland, including three in a row from 1904 to 1906. Twice she defeated Florence in the finals. She won her first title in 1899 and her second in 1902. She defeated Florence in 1907 in Newcastle, Ireland, by a score of 2 and 1.[9] She also won the British Ladies Amateur Championship in 1902 and finished runner-up to Rhona Adair in 1904.

In the 1908 Irish championships, the entire female side of the Hezlet family dominated the event. The *New York Times* wrote during the event, "The Hezlet family stands unique for the number of women golfers that it can furnish for notable competitions."

May published an influential book on women's golf in 1904 entitled *Ladies Golf*.

BEATRIX HOYT

Prodigies are not new to women's sports. Gymnastics saw the rise of Olga Korbut, Nadia Comaneche, and America's own dynamo Mary Lou Retton. Tennis greats Monica Seles, Martina Hingis, and Jennifer Capriati stormed the nets at an early age, making their mark on grand-slam tournaments with their precocious yet powerful strokes. Golf is no exception.

In the 1890s a young 16-year-old girl named Beatrix Hoyt won three straight U.S. national women's golf championships. What makes Hoyt's accomplishments even more amazing is that she starting playing only 2 years before her first national championship victory. In 1896, she came to the tournament, predicting a victory. The event at Morristown, New Jersey, was held in front of a "large and enthusiastic crowd of spectators."[10]

The *New York Times* reported: "It was rather odd, however, to see this deeply tanned girl beat women many years her senior and with more experience in the game."[11] She had to navigate through a field of twenty-five players, including Miss Anna Sands, the sister of William H. Sands, the amateur champion of the St. Andrews Golf Club. In the quarterfinals, she dispatched Miss F.H. McLane 8 and 6 to set up a semifinal showdown with Miss Sands. Hoyt won that match and then defeated Mrs. Arthur Turnure 2 and 1 for the championship.

F.W. Crane gushed in praise over the 16-year-old's triumph:

The victory of Miss Beatrix Hoyt, the sixteen-year-old girl from the Shinnecock Hills Golf Club, stands as one of the most remarkable incidents of the entire golf year. Miss Hoyt has been playing barely two years, but her game is characterized by a steadiness and precision that would be considered charming even in an older and more experienced golfer.[12]

She teamed with William Sands to win the mixed foursome tournament at Westchester Country Club in New York in November 1897. The pair defeated their nearest rivals by seven strokes—97 to 104.[13]

After her third straight triumph in 1898, the *New York Times* reported: "It would seem by her career on the golf links as though Miss Hoyt was invincible."[14] It surely seemed that way to her opponents. Hoyt had early exposure to the golf courses, as her parents lived on the grounds of the West-chester Country Club in Westchester, New York. She retired in 1990 at the age of 19 after losing to Margaret Curtis in the semifinals of a tournament in 1900.

THE CURTIS SISTERS

Margaret and Harriet Curtis were dominant American players. Their cousin Lawrence was a president of the United States Tennis Association. The 13-year-old Margaret made an impact at the U.S. amateur championship in 1895 and later dethroned the great Beatrix Hoyt in 1900. She won the U.S. amateurs in 1907, 1910, and 1911. Her sister Harriet was nearly as accomplished, winning the U.S. title in 1906.

Unfortunately, the Curtis sisters at times could not best the very best players on the British Isles. In May 1907, the two ventured to Newcastle, Ireland, to challenge their counterparts. In the third round, Harriet dropped a match to Violet Hezlet, while Margaret fell to former two-time British champion May Hezlet and fell 3 shots down with 2 holes to play. (In golf parlance, she lost 3 and 2.)

The sisters' names are forever enshrined into golf lore with the prestigious Curtis Cup named after them. The Cup is awarded to the winning team of golfers between the United States and Great Britain. Margaret and Harriet officially presented a silver cup to be given to the winners. In May 1931 the competition was announced with some referring to it as the "feminine equivalent of the classic Walker Cup."[15] The Curtis sisters announced the silver cup as the competition's trophy. However, the Ladies' Golf Union declined the silver cup with regret. The USGA president Herbert Ramsey attempted to deflect any potential controversy, saying: "Since it is a matter of policy with the British women, we can have no controversy."[16] Later the British reversed their stance and agreed to accept the Cup in 1934 if they won. No official announcement was made explaining the change in policy.[17]

DOROTHY CAMPBELL

Dorothy Campbell dominated international golf during the first part of the twentieth century, winning ten national championships in England,

Scotland, Canada, and the United States. She won the Scottish Ladies Championship in 1905, 1906, and 1908. She captured the U.S. Women's Amateur Championship in 1909, 1910, and 1924. She won three straight Canadian Ladies Opens from 1910 to 1912 after moving to Canada. She did not defend her Canadian crown in 1913 because she had married Pittsburgh steel magnate Jack Vandervort Hurd. They later divorced in the 1920s.

Born in Edinburgh, Scotland, in 1883, she began playing golf when she was 5 years old although she had swung a golf club at only 18 months. She played on the local town links where her grandfather and eight uncles played. She developed into a great player after she changed her swing from a half-swing to a full-swing.

In 1909 she won her first U.S. Women's Amateur Championship by defeating Mrs. R.H. Barlow 3 and 2 in a thrilling match in Philadelphia. According to the Associated Press, "Miss Campbell gave one of the best exhibitions of the game ever shown by a woman in an American tournament."[18]

She retained the U.S. crown the next year with another narrow victory over England's Mrs. O.M. Martin. Campbell prevailed by a narrow score of 2 and 1. Perhaps her greatest triumph occurred in August 1924 at the U.S. Women's Championship when she was 40 years old. Dorothy Campbell Hurd was not favored in the championship, as she had been passed by the great American star Glenna Collett, Edith Cummings, and several other younger players. However, experience proved the difference in the match-play competition. In the finals Hurd defeated tennis champion Mary K. Browne 7 and 6 to capture her third national U.S. title. The Associated Press kindly reported that "the experience of a veteran of the links...told against the novice."[19] Hurd later married Edward Lee Howe, chairman of the Princeton, N.J. Bank and Trust Co. They eventually divorced.

Campbell died when she fell beneath an Atlantic Coast Line train in Yemasee, South Carolina. She was 62 years old.

ALEXA STIRLING

> I played with her later and was greatly struck by her beautiful style of play, the neatness and deliberation of swing and the gracefulness of her poise in playing the shots.
>
> —Joyce Wethered[20]

Another great female American golfer was Alexa Stirling of Atlanta. Writing for the *Atlanta Constitution,* all-time great Bobby Jones wrote: "Alexa Stirling, with whom I have played for years, is small, but wiry, and possesses unusual stamina for a woman."[21] Jones had cause for optimism after playing with Stirling during a "Dixie Kids" tour during World War I to raise money for the Red Cross. Jones should have respect for Stirling, as she often defeated him when they were kids—though Stirling was 5 years older.[22]

Stirling won three straight U.S. national championships. She captured her first title in 1915 before World War I caused the cancellation of the tournament for 2 years in 1916–17. After the war ended, Stirling returned to dominance on the links, capturing the title in 1919 and 1920. She finished second in 1921, 1923, and 1925.

Jones wrote his praise of Stirling on the eve of the 1921 British women's championship when the dominant figure in the game was British champion Cecil Leitch whom Jones noted could outdrive most men players. Jones realized that Leitch was the odds-on favorite, but added: "I don't exactly know the playing abilities of the other American and Canadian girls in the tournament, but I believe that if anyone from our side of the water wins, it will be Alexa Stirling of Atlanta."[23]

EDITH CUMMINGS

On August 25, 1924, *Time Magazine* featured the first woman on its cover. She was known other than the striking golfer Edith Cummings. She burst onto the national scene a year earlier when she upset Alex Stirling to win the 1923 U.S. Women's National Championship. Chuck Evans of the *Los Angeles Times* wrote of her: "The victory of Miss Edith Cummings I the women's national championship this year has done much to popularize women's golf in this country."[24]

She later married Curtis Munson and lived a life that the *Washington Post* described as one that could be depicted in a Katherine Hepburn movie.[25] In her later life she became a wealthy benefactor, setting up foundations and giving to charity. Her name lives on through the Edith Cummings Munson Golf Award that is presented annually at the NGCA (National Golf Coaches Association) Awards Banquet at the NCAA Division I Championship. The award goes to the student-athlete who is both a NGCA All-American Scholar and an NGCA All-American.[26]

VIRGINIA VAN WIE

Virginia Van Wie was one of America's greatest golfers in the 1920s and 1930s. She made her name at the U.S. Women's Amateur Championships where she won three consecutive times from 1932 to 1934. She may have added more titles, but she retired at the relatively young age of 1925 and became a golf instructor.

Born in 1909, Van Wie took up golf at the age of fourteen and played competitively on the national scene for 12 years. She gave golf lessons from 1950 until she retired in 1975.[27]

MAUREEN ORCUTT

Maureen Orcutt was known as "the Duchess of Golf." She was a topflight amateur golfer in the early 1920s who won sixty-five major events during her playing career. Along with Collett Vare, Virginia Van Wie, and Helen Hicks, she was known as part of the "Big Four" of Women's Golf.

She won the 1925 Eastern Women's Amateur Championship in 1925, 1928, and 1929. She won the Canadian Women's Amateur in 1929 and 1930. Many years later in 1962 she won the USGA Senior Women's Amateur Championship. She could never win the coveted U.S. Women's Amateur Championship, although she came close in 1927 and 1936 when she finished second. Fellow golf journalist Gordon White said of Orcutt: "The thing about Maureen is her renown. She would hit the ball as far any woman in the world could hit it. Maureen was a big woman, quite strong. She wasn't at all fat. She really could bust one. That was one of her primary strengths."[28]

Orcutt became a pioneer in women's sports journalism when she took a sportswriting position with the *New York Times* in 1937. She often had to write about actual golf sporting events that she played.

Born in 1907, Orcutt learned golf at the age of ten and was a highly decorated athlete as a youngster. She was the star of her local basketball team before turning her focus to the links. The great golf writer Rhonda Glenn summed up Orcutt best when she wrote: "What one famous novelist wrote in his classic American novel could have just as easily been written about Orcutt as she gracefully became one of the game's *grande dames.* "She was a golfer," F. Scott Fitzgerald wrote in *The Great Gatsby,* "and everyone knew her name."[29]

She died in January 2007 at the age of 99.

HELEN HICKS

Helen Hicks was one of the great women golfers of the 1920s, 1930s, and 1940s. She won the 1929 Canadian Open, the 1931 U.S. Women's Amateur, the 1937 Western Open, and the 1940 Titleholders Championship. She burst onto the national scene in March 1929 as a high schooler from Hempstead, New York, by defeating the great Glenna Collett Vare 2 and 1 in the semifinals of the U.S. Women's national championship. What made the win even more remarkable was that she had suffered from food poisoning a day earlier. She lost in the finals to Virginia Van Wie by a score of 3 and 2.

Later that year she won a 72-hole medal play classic in Chicago with a fourteen-stroke victory over Van Wie, Maureen Orcutt, and the rest of the field. Sportswriter Paul R. Michelson gushed: "Compared with women's par, Miss Hicks's performance probably established a new record for feminine golf."[30]

In 1931, the 20-year-old Hicks defeated three-time defending champion Glenna Collett Vare to win the U.S. Women's Amateur by a score of 2 and 1. She turned the tide on the 14th hole with a pitch shot that landed right near the hole. The *Chicago Daily Tribune* reported: "Every championship has its miraculous shots, its pulsating minutes, and its touches of drama, but Miss Hicks merged them all into one as she pitched that shot to the green."[31] A gracious ex-champion Collett Vare said: "She has stamped herself as a champion."[32]

Hicks also doubled as a sportswriter, writing about the firth round of the British Women's Open golf championship in May 1932. She recounted her narrow loss in match play to Doris Park of Scotland, writing: "After losing at the sixteenth hole, I cannot say that I feel too badly, even though I had my eye on the championship this year because I lost to a good player and was playing well myself."[33]

In 1935 Hicks retired from amateur golf and turned professional to become "America's first business woman golfer." She turned professional by accepting a position with Wilson-Westing sports goods company in Chicago as its women's golf department adviser. "Naturally I'm unhappy over the fact that I am giving up all competitive golf activity, but on the other hand I believe that with my knowledge of golf and the sincere co-operation I am getting, I am going to be able to do a lot of things I have wanted to do along the line of developing golf among women and girls."[34]

She predicted that other girls would soon follow her into the professional ranks: "I think that in the next two or three years there will be a great field for women golf professionals."[35] She later said that she had no regrets about her turn to the professional ranks, saying "I wouldn't consider taking back amateur standing if I had to give up what I have now."[36]

As a professional she made her marks on the links by winning the Western Open Golf championship by defeating Beatrice Barrett of Minnesota by a score of 6 and 5. She became the first women golf professional to win a significant golfing event.[37]

She was a driving force in the efforts to create a women's professional golf tour similar to the men's PGA (Professional Golf Association). Her proposed organization, which was supported by fellow professional Patty Berg, would have two main purposes:

- Promotion of golf among women through exhibitions and demonstrations. Physical education teachers in schools who instruct their classes in golf fundamentals will become auxiliary members.
- Provision of a wide range tournament program. In order to guarantee a representative field, the tournaments would have to be open affairs, making both pros and amateurs eligible.[38]

Helen Hicks later became one of the original thirteen founding members of the LPGA. Past her playing prime by that time, she generally was not able to match the golfing abilities of players such as Babe Zaharias or Patty Berg. She passed away in 1974.

OPAL HILL

Arguably Mrs. Opal Hill owed her life to the game of golf. Doctors had told her that a kidney infection she contracted after giving birth to a child was life threatening. They recommended a healthy dose of exercise. Hill responded by becoming more active and religiously pursued the game of golf. She not only became healthy but also became a championship-level golfer.

She won the Western Amateur three times, in 1929, 1931, and 1932. She also won the Western Open in 1935 and 1936. Married to attorney Oscar Hill, she had a nursing degree. In September 1937, at the age of 45, she shot a round of 66 to win the Missouri Women's golf championship for the third year in a row. Her 66 consisted of a hole-in-one and two eagles. At the time it was believed to be the best round ever turned in by a woman in a competitive tournament.[39]

ENID WILSON

Enid Wilson had one of the most fascinating lives and careers of golf's early greats. Born in Stonebroom, England, in 1910, Wilson was a very mischievous child. At the age of four, she removed the heads of all her father's golf clubs. At boarding school, officials expelled her for being a "damned nuisance."[40] Wilson claimed it was for her cursing at a school official who curtailed her time on the golf course. She didn't mind being expelled from school because it gave her more time on the golf course—which she used to great advantage.

At seventeen, she finished second in the English Ladies' Championship and won the title in 1928 and 1930. At the peak of her golfing prowess, she won three straight British Open Championships from 1931 to 1933. She may have won several more titles and continued her dominance if not for an untimely ruling by the Ladies' Golf Union. That austere body declared her to be a "non-amateur" because she had made money off golf by writing captions to a series of golfing photographs. Wilson had to retire from competitive amateur golf as a result of this ruling.[41] Years later, Wilson said she held no bitterness for the decision then and now: "Lots of people thought that perhaps I bore the Ladies' Golf Union a grudge for sort of consigning me to limbo. Not in the slightest, never have done. I knew perfectly well what I was up to. I had no desire to play any more serious golf. I'd had my fill of it."[42]

The ruling did not stop Wilson from remaining a force in the game of golf. She coauthored a textbook on how to play the game. She later became a women's golf correspondent with the *Daily Telegraph*. "The appointment proved a tremendous boon for the ladies' game," reads a 2006 article in the *Derby Evening Telegraph*. "As well as keeping her readers entertained, Enid also championed advances in the sport."[43]

Wilson later authored a book entitled *A Gallery of Women Golfers*, which contained biographies of many leading female golfers. For some reason she excluded herself. She should not have given her accomplishments.

Wilson died at the age of 85 in January 1996.

GLENNA COLLETT VARE

> Of all the great players I have known, Glenna presents the most detached of attitudes in playing a match. She intrudes her presence to the smallest degree upon her opponents. I would even say that she appears to withdraw herself almost entirely from everything except the game, and her shots alone remind one of the brilliant adversary one is up against. If she is finding her true form then there is little hope, except by a miracle, of surviving—at any rate in an eighteen-hole match.
>
> —Joyce Wethered[44]

Known as the Queen of American Golf, Glenna Collett Vare is considered the greatest American golfer of the first part of the twentieth century. Born in New Haven, Connecticut, in 1903, she did not start playing golf until she turned fourteen. She received expert instruction, however, from former British Open champion Alex Smith at the Metacomet Club.

She won the U.S. Women's Amateur tournament a record six times: in 1922, 1925, 1928, 1929, 1930, and 1935. Her last victory was a bridge of golfing generations as she narrowly defeated a 17-year-old dynamo named Patricia Jean Berg.

She also won two Canadian Amateur titles in 1923 and 1924 and added a French Amateur title in 1925. Her most dominant year was 1924, when she won 59 out of 60 matches. The only player she seemingly could not beat was perhaps the greatest player of all time—Joyce Wethered. However, even Wethered spoke wonders for Vare's game, writing in her book *Golfing Memories and Methods:* "If she is finding her true form, then there is little hope, except by miracle, of surviving." The great Byron Nelson called her the best of all time: "Mrs. Glenna Collett Vare of Philadelphia probably was the greatest woman golfer of all time. Mrs. Vare set some kind of record when she won the national women's championship six times. She was a stylist in all departments of the game."[45]

She died at the age of 85 in 1989, but her name lives on the modern LPGA tour as every year the golfer with the lowest scoring average on tour is bestowed the Vare Trophy.

— CHAPTER 3 —

JOYCE WETHERED—THE GREATEST FEMALE GOLFER EVER

Joyce Wethered was one of the greatest golfers, man or woman, of all time, because she made herself understand the game technically, had the ability to put that knowledge into practice and had the strength to conquer and subdue any doubts from within. Sometimes, she suffered greatly, but her secret was to control such emotions until after the work was done and the championship won.

—Basil Ashton Tinkler[1]

Golfing great Gene Sarazen was asked to list the top-ten male and female golfers of all time for a 1982 article for *Golf Digest.* Among the men, he listed the name of Jack Nicklaus—a name that still resonates with even the casual sports fan. The name Nicklaus is known by thousands who have never even picked up a golf club. Among the women, Sarazen listed the name of Joyce Wethered.[2] Unfortunately, not even many avid golfers have ever heard the name of Joyce Wethered.

By many historians account, Joyce Wethered was the greatest female golfer to ever pick up a golf club. Her greatest early rival, Cecil Leitch, wrote about her: "She is absolutely at home with any club, and the game is no trouble to her....She never knows when she is beaten; in fact she appears to be at her best when down."[3]

Her dominance impressed not only her female rivals but also the great male golfers of her generation. No less an authority than Walter Hagen wrote of Wethered: "When she is playing only mediocre stuff for her, she can still give strokes to any woman golfer in the world. When she is at the top of her game, there is not another woman player in the same class."[4]

The great Bobby Jones said it best for *American Golfer* in 1930: "I have no hesitancy in saying that, accounting for the unavoidable handicap of a woman's lesser physical strength, she is the finest golfer I have ever seen."[5]

It was surprising that Wethered became such a golfing great given that her parents worried she was too weak to attend school and insisted on home-schooling her. She also had only one formal golf lesson in her early years. But she came from a family very interested in golf and one of economic means.

She burst onto the golfing scene as a young 18-year-old in 1920 at Sherington for the British national championship. Entering the tournament, she was known only for being her brother's younger sister. Roger Wethered was one of the finest male players in England. He would later win the country's amateur championship in 1923. Joyce was in her brother's shadow at the time. She entered the tournament as the number-six-rated player on the Surrey county team. The format for the tournament called for an opening elimination round, which would set the top sixty-four players. Similar to today's NCAA basketball tournaments, these players would then participate in match-play until the final two competed for the championship.

Wethered managed to make it through to the final, where she faced the dominating Leitch. In the final match, Leitch started quickly and jumped out to a 4-hole lead through the first 9 holes. However, Wethered played better on the back 9 and squared the match. She managed to hole a putt on the seventeenth green to capture the championship. It was Leitch's first loss in match-play format in nearly 7 years. Wethered recognized that she had pulled an upset, writing years later: "Though I finally won the match and the championship by two and one, it cannot be denied that the result was the biggest surprise that ladies' golf has ever had sprung upon it."[6]

In 1921, Leitch returned with a vengeance, defeating Joyce in the finals of both the British and the French championships. In June 1921 in Turnberry, Scotland, she won 4 and 3 (4 holes up with only 3 holes to play) to capture the British title. Later that month, the two archrivals competed for the French championship in Fontainebleau. It was Wethered's first trip across the sea, but she still managed to play well enough to reach the final. In the semifinals, Wethered ousted American star Alexa Stirling 5 and 4, while Leitch managed to squeak by Miss Molly Griffiths 1-up. In the 36-hole final, Leitch raced out to a 7-hole advantage. Wethered could not stage a rally and Leitch captured the championship by a score of 7 and 6.

Alexa Stirling evaluated her British competitors in a piece for the *Atlanta Constitution*, praising them for their superior play. With prescience, Stirling wrote: "To my mind Miss Wethered is going to give Miss Leitch a very close run for premier honors."[7] She continued with her effusive praise of Joyce: "Like her brother, she rises at times to heights of great brilliance and it is never safe to say that she is beaten while there is still any chance for her at all."[8]

Stirling's words proved accurate, as Wethered ended Leitch's reign as the world's dominant female player in 1922. In fact, the 1921 French championship was the last time that Leitch managed to defeat her younger opponent.

Wethered smarted from those two defeats to Cecil Leitch. She vowed to improve her own game and become the world's best. Her biographer Basil Tinkler writes of the 1921 defeat at the French championship: "It was a thumping and Joyce knew it and she did not hesitate to acknowledge that Cecil was much the better player in every department of the game."[9]

Joyce's hard work paid off in 1922, as she established herself as the game's dominant force. In May in Sandwich, England, the two titans of women's golf once again marched through the match-play format to the finals. Interest in the match exceeded that of any previous women's golf match. Sports fans love rivalries and, particularly, rivalries with opponents of contrasting styles. Leitch was a pure power player, while Wethered was a stylist and master putter.

Wethered defeated Joan Stocker by a score of 5 and 4. Leitch was equally impressive, topping the talented Gladys Bastin by the same score of 5 and 4. Many experts predicted that the 20-year-old Wethered would give Leitch a good match though Leitch still entered the championship as the favorite. Her two head-to-head finals victories the previous year cemented her place at the top of the game.

No one could have expected the lopsided nature of the 36-hole final. For the morning's 18 holes, the two golfers battled to a virtual standstill. Both golfers fired 84s, with Wethered winning 6 holes and Leitch 5. The afternoon round was much different. Wethered bested her opponent in 7 of the first 9 holes, including 4 straight. Through the first 9 holes, Wethered fired a formidable 39, while Leitch stumbled in with a 47. The match ended after the 27th hole with Wethered winning 9 up and 7 to play. The Associated Press reported: "Miss Cecil Leitch suffered the most overwhelming defeat ever administered to a finalist since British championship golf matches were inaugurated."[10]

The torch had been passed, as Joyce never turned back from that 1922 performance. She proceeded to dominate women's golf as no player had ever done. She even took time that year to coauthor a book on golf with her brother Roger, entitled *Golf on Both Sides*. She won the English Ladies Championship that year, besting Joan Stocker easily in the finals.

In 1923, Wethered suffered an upset at the hands of Mrs. Alan MacBeth in the semifinals of the British Ladies Open Championship. MacBeth shocked the golfing world by sinking a birdie on the 17th hole to win 2 and 1. It was one of only two defeats Wethered would suffer the entire year.

In 1924, she stormed back in Portrush, Ireland, to regain the British Open crown. In an earlier round she dispatched Leitch 6 and 4. In the finals, she overwhelmed an overmatched Mrs. F. Cautley 7 and 6. She displayed similar dominance in the 1924 English championships, defeating Dolly Fowler

8 and 7. "It was all so unfair," wrote her biographer Basil Tinkler. "This woman was not real. She was certainly in a class of her own."[11]

The 1925 British open featured a field of more than 100 female golfers, including the best from several countries all gathered in Troon, Scotland. The Associated Press referred to it as "the most cosmolitan gathering of feminine golfers ever assembled."[12] The United States sent their best hope since Alexa Stirling—a young woman named Glenna Collett. Experts considered her perhaps the best threat to dethrone Joyce Wethered.

As fate would have it, the dream matchup occurred in the third round, as the tournament draw was random, rather than seeded as the match-play championships of today. The match drew an eager crowd of 5,000 to watch the two friendly players duel on the golf course. Glenna played valiantly but succumbed to Joyce by a score of 4 and 3. Glenna cabled her father George after the match: "I lost 4 and 3. Joyce played unbeatable golf. I am sorry Dad."[13] Glenna had nothing but praise for her rival, saying that in the afternoon round Joyce would have taken any player in the world, including the great Walter Hagen: "Hagen, would have been hard put to it to beat Miss Wethered, so what chance had I of winning?"[14]

Los Angeles Times correspondent said Wethered played "machine-like golf," capitalizing on every mistake by her American opponent. He described Wethered as being "as cool as an iceberg and just as relentless."[15]

Wethered marched through the field to the final round where she faced her old nemesis Cecil Leitch. The 33-year-old Leitch summoned all her will and skill to produce what would be one of the great match-play final rounds in the history of the game. After the first 18 holes, the two legends were dead even. Wethered managed to take a 2-hole with only 2 holes to play. It appeared to the nearly 10,000 in attendance that the coronation would continue. However, Leitch won the 17th and 18th holes of the afternoon session to square the match dead even after 36 holes. The two women proceeded to the 37th hole for sudden death. Leitch missed the green and managed to shoot only a 5. Wethered found the green and sank a 3-ft putt for the win.

Amazingly, only a month after this historic win, Wethered retired from championship golf. Perhaps the mental strain of being number one had caught up with her. Perhaps she just wanted a break and some relaxation. Whatever the exact reason, she famously told the *Daily Express*:

I have no reason that would appeal to the masculine mind. I am stopping playing simply because I choose to. I am tired of it for the time being. There is no mystery about it. I am not going to emigrate or marry; I have simply exercised a woman's prerogative of doing something without the slightest regard for anybody thinks and because I want to please myself.[16]

The Associated Press called her "the empress of golf." She retired at the tender age of twenty-three—at the top of the sporting world.

Wethered still played golf but only recreationally. She pursued her many other interests, including tennis and several winter sports in Switzerland. However, she still made international news with her golfing exploits, including a story that became the lore of legend. Apparently, she was playing at the Sheringham course—the site of one of her national championships—when she had a key putt on the 17th hole. Just as she leaned over her 9-ft putt, a train roared by a mere 100 yards away, disturbing players throughout the golf course. However, Wethered proceeded as if nothing was happening and holed the 9-ft putt. Her playing partner asked her how she maintained her concentration as the train roared nearby. She allegedly replied, "What train?"[17]

Wethered missed competitive golf more than she must have thought, for she returned to a doubles match in March 1927 at Addington in the London ladies' foursome tournament. Partnered with Mrs. Kennedy, she prevailed over Miss Purling and Mrs. Glen by a single hole.

In 1929, Wethered returned to singles competition when she entered the British Open at the historic St. Andrews course in Scotland. As she said in her autobiography *Golfing Memories and Methods:* "The appeal of St. Andrews where the championship of 1929 was to be played proved too irresistible."[18] Joyce returned to the game of competitive golf because of her love for St. Andrews and perhaps because many encouraged her to win the crown for the British from the American invasion. Many anticipated a clash between Wethered and Collett. As the Associated Press reported, "all eyes today were for Glenna and Joyce....[C]lose observers expect these two to go on to the 36-hole final."[19]

The two easily survived their first matches: Collett defeated Marjorie White by a score of 5 and 3, while Wethered topped Phyllis Lobbelt 6 and 5. The much anticipated matchup became reality on May 17, 1929. "Almost everyone had the final which they wanted," Tinkler wrote. "Joyce Wethered v. Glenna Collett; Great Britain v. the United States of America; the queen of English golf v. the queen of American golf. A fiction writer could not have set it up better."[20]

Collett was a serious challenger to Wethered's title as world's best female golfer. She had won the American championship numerous times since her first title in 1922. She had won major titles in France and Ireland. For her career she won forty-nine championships. On May 17, she looked for all the world like she would become the first American to capture the British crown, as she moved 5-up after the first 9 holes. Collett was playing incredible golf, posting an incredible score of 34 through the first 9. Joyce later wrote: "Glenna's first nine holes of the match was the finest sequence of holes I have ever seen a lady play."[21]

Ever the champion, Wethered began creeping back into the match. Collett began to finally miss some putts, while the English champion returned to form. The result was that Collett's lead after the first 18 holes was only 2 up.

In the afternoon round, Wethered struck early, evening the match after the third hole. The English champion played the first 9 holes of the afternoon session in a 35, while Collett faltered. Wethered ended up prevailing by a score of 3 and 1. Writer Henry C. Crouch reported for the *New York Times:* "It was a great fight from first to last and throughout the two rivals showed the finest sporting spirit and fortitude, considering the somewhat unruly attitude of the crowd against which they had to contend."[22]

The admiring crowd roared and rowdied after the great matchup that Wethered and Collett Vare were separated. Wethered recalled:

It was almost impossible to ignore the pent-up excitement of the crowd which was ready to break out as soon as the last putt was struck. When the moment finally came it threatened very nearly to destroy us. Glenna and I were torn apart and became the centre of a squeezing, swaying, and almost hysterical mob, shouting and cheering themselves hoarse.[23]

Wethered accomplished her goal of becoming the game's greatest golfer and decided shortly after her triumphs in 1929 that she would not play more championship golf. She announced in February 1930 that she would not defend her British Open championship and would retire permanently from championship golf.

That did not mean, however, that Joyce quit playing golf. Instead, she played all sorts of exhibitions—often times against male golfers. In May 1930 she played a four-ball match with her brother Roger, the great American golfer Bobby Jones, and the male amateur player T. A. Bourn. Jones and Bourn scored 75, Joyce a 76, and her brother an 80. After golfing with Joyce, Jones remarked that he had never played with any golfer—man or woman—who struck a golf ball better. Her biographer Basil Tinkler writes that Joyce and Jones had mutual admiration for their playing styles, writing that "both had a long, flowing, apparently effortless swing which was a joy to behold, particularly when they were playing with someone who preferred to propel the ball by force, and achieve much less."[24]

In June 1930, Wethered defeated male golfer Cyril J. H. Tolley in a matchup that featured some unusual rules. The rules called for female players to receive a two-stroke advantage and drove the ball from a closer tee. Still, Wethered finished two strokes ahead of her male counterpart.[25]

Wethered still played international golf but only in team matches. In 1931, she participated in the first clash between French golfers and British/ Irish golfers. The British ladies proved too fierce, defeating their opponents 8.5 to .5. Joyce seemingly had lost none of her touch, winning in a four-ball match with her partner Mrs. Garon by a score of 7 and 6 over two overmatched French women.

This international clash whetted the public's appetite for an even more interesting clash. Margaret Curtis, the great American golfer who lost to her British counterparts in the 1905 clash, had long desired a chance to create an annual event between U.S. and British lady golfers. The event eventually led to the awarding of a silver cup to the winning team—appropriate named the Curtis Cup. The Curtis Cup's Web site explains: "The cup, a silver bowl of Paul Revere design, is inscribed, 'To stimulate friendly rivalry among the women golfers of many lands.' The cup was first presented in 1927 to give momentum to the competition, but play didn't begin until 1932, largely because of financial reasons."[26]

The historic match was played at Wentworth Golf Club, in England. The formidable American team, captained by Marion Hollins, featured players such as Maureen Orcutt, Virginia Van Wie, Opal Hill, and Helen Hicks. Wethered captained the British team, though she was more suited to her role as a dominant player. Reticent by nature, she did not fit the mold of the 'rah-rah' type captain. Her team included Wanda Morgan, Enid Wilson, Diana Fishwick, and Elsie Corlett.

The match included three sets of foursomes and six singles matches. The Americans played better during four ball, prevailing in all three of the doubles matches and ended up prevailing by a final score of 5.5 to 3.5. Wethered played well during the singles round. She defeated her American rival Collett by a score of 6 and 4. Helen Hicks, an American player, wrote about the match for the *New York Times*. She praised Wethered's singles play, writing that she "played as good golf as she has ever played in her life."[27] Hicks referred to the "obviously superior play" of her team but acknowledged that "honestly" they did not expect to win all three foursomes. She spoke probably for all of the players when she added: "This being the first formal women's International match, we were naturally extremely happy to come out of the fray with victory. We all hope these matches will be continued in future years."[28]

Some criticized the British team and, apparently, Wethered for failing to develop better team camaraderie. One account quoted a British golf authority as saying: "Mrs. Vare will never beat Miss Wethered but Britain will never beat America until team spirit is cultivated."[29]

Wethered's career took a different direction after she took a job as a golf adviser to Fortnam & Mason's Piccadilly Store in London. This action of taking a job "astonished" golf officials with the LGU (Ladies Golf Union) who said the action may impact her amateur status.[30] The official rules of the LGU adhered to the standard articulated by the Royal and Ancient St., the supreme golf body in Great Britain. That standard provides that an amateur golfer is one who has not received money for playing or teaching the game or "because of skill as a golfer has not received salary or remuneration either directly or indirectly or individually from any firm dealing in goods relating to the playing of the game."[31]

This issue of amateur or professional status became a huge issue in Great Britain not only over Wethered but also because of Enid Wilson, another

British Open champion. In 1934, the LGU refused Wilson's entry for the British championship because she violated a rule that prohibited women golfers from writing for newspapers unless they were journalists by trade. When informed of the decision, Wilson responded that she was "through with golf forever."[32]

Wethered never again competed for amateur titles but still made national and international headlines for her golf play. She never attempted to challenge the British golf rules.

The strict rules for female amateur golfers hurt the British squad when they traveled across the ocean in 1934 to Chevy Chase, Maryland, to seek revenge in the next Curtis Club match. Without Wethered and Wilson, the British squad was beaten even more soundly 6.5 to 2.5. In fact, the British did not win a Curtis Cup match against the Americans until 1952 in Muirfield, Scotland.

In 1935, she toured the United States, playing a highly publicized series of exhibitions with top female and male U.S. golfers, including Bobby Jones and Gene Sarazen. Wethered anxiously looked forward to playing with and against some of the great American players, including the male stars. Part of the excitement stemmed from the fact that she had never crossed the Atlantic Ocean to visit the United States. The *New York Times* reported: "She had never been further away from her native shores than the south of France, so that this is a real adventure."[33]

In July 1935, Wethered joined with Freddy McLeod to defeat her favorite rival, Glenna Collett Vare and Roland MacKenzie 3 and 1. Wethered fired an 80, while Collett Vare shot an 83. Later in the month, Wethered played with Horton Smith to defeat the great Gene Sarazen and a powerful athletic woman named Mildred "Babe" Didrikson. Wethered shot a respectable 78, while the Babe fired an 88. The "Babe" was "a mute wild throughout her round," reported one account of the match.[34]

Later that month, Sarazen and the "Babe" had another chance against the "Great Lady of Golf." In Buffalo, New York, Wethered and club pro Elwyn Nagell defeated the American duo. Wethered fired a 77, while the Babe shot an 81. The great Byron Nelson later wrote that Wethered's American exhibition tour "did a great deal to stimulate interest in women's golf."[35]

Wethered also played exhibitions in her native land. In Northwood England, in April 1936, Wethered participated in a series of matches of great U.S. and British golfers. Wethered and Marion Miley faced off against Enid Wilson and a young American from Minnesota named Patty Berg. Wilson and Berg triumphed 5 and 4. Later Wethered and Mrs. Frank Goldthwaite defeated Wilson and Collett Vare 4 and 3. Wethered stole the show with a display of golf that caused Collett Vare to exclaim, "That kind of golf simply isn't fair."[36] The two stars of this particular matchup were Wethered and Berg, an individual that the golfing world would hear much more from in subsequent decades. The Associated Press reported that the two "stole the show" in the exhibition with their masterful short games.[37]

Joyce faded from the golfing world after marrying Sir John Heathcoat-Amory at St. George's Church in Hanover Square in January 6, 1937. The wedding party included Roger Wethered and none other than Cecil Leitch. After her wedding, "golf took a back seat in her life."[38]

Golf historians rank Wethered as among the greats of the games. As with all sports, it is virtually impossible to compare athletes of different eras. You hear it all the time in boxing, for example, whether Rocky Marciano could beat Mike Tyson, whether Joe Louis would beat Muhammad Ali. The same applies to women's golf. Who knows if Wethered would beat Annika Sorenstam. Wethered used inferior equipment and did not have the same training facilities. There are many who vouch that Wethered was the greatest golfer who ever lived—the so-called "First Lady of Golf," the "Bobby Jones of women's golf," and similar appellations.

Whether she was the greatest golfer of all time is a debatable question, but she may well have lived the longest among all the great champions. Wethered passed away in November 1997 the day after her ninety-sixth birthday.

—— CHAPTER 4 ——

THE BABE AND THE BERG...AND LOUISE SUGGS

In 1974, the World Golf Hall of Fame admitted thirteen golfers—eleven men and only two women. Those two women were Mildred "Babe" Didrikson Zaharias and Patricia Jean Berg. Selected by the Golf Writers Association, the two women took their place with such golfing legends as Arnold Palmer, Byron Nelson, Sam Snead, Ben Hogan, Bobby Jones, and Jack Nicklaus.

MILDRED "BABE" DIDRIKSON ZAHARIAS

But I can't shake the suspicion that the Babe, on any given day, could beat any of them by sheer force of will. She had that special quality of champions. She could be as good as she had to be....Babe was a grand showman. She had a flair for the dramatic and a raw, earthly sense of humor. She loved life and loved people. She loved the color and the glory of the passing parade and wore her role of champion as naturally as Walter Hagen did....

I never expect to see another one like her. Some day I suppose another woman super athlete will come along to send another generation of sports-writers digging back into the yellowing pages of the record books to make a comparison. But it will be a long time after your time and mine.

—Fred Corcoran[1]

Ask most sports experts the greatest woman athlete of all-time and most will mention the name of Babe Didrikson Zaharias. Mildred, better known as "the Babe," was dominant in every sport she played—and she played many of them. She starred in basketball during her early years, dominating in high school and then for a women's industrial league where she earned all-American honors. She played every sport imaginable and mastered them all. Every sport she tried, she seemingly became great. James F. Fowler wrote: "Eight months after she first took up tennis she beat Alice Marble and Big Bill Tilden. She could have been a championship swimmer and diver, bowler and soccer player. She out-pitched the great Satchel Paige and has played with professional men's baseball teams."[2] In 1950, a group of sportswriters voted on the female athlete of the half-century. Didrikson received 319 first-place votes and a total of 1,030 points. Her nearest competitor, tennis legend Helen Wills Moody, received 20 first-place votes and 334 total points for a distant second. Even the great racehorse Secretariat did not blow out the competition as the Babe did during his great honor.

Born in 1911 to Norwegian immigrants, Mildred grew up in the seaside town of Port Arthur, Texas. Her father Ole worked as a seaman and a cabinetmaker though sometimes he did not hold a full-time job, placing the family in tough economic times. Her mother called her youngest daughter Mildred "Babe" because the Norwegian word *baden* meant "baby" in English. Babe would later brag that her nickname came because she could hit a baseball like the great New York Yankees slugger William Herman "Babe" Ruth. Her biographer Susan E. Cayleff explained: "She told this story often that it stuck, even though it wasn't true."[3]

A hurricane damaged the Didrikson home, which caused Babe's mother Hannah to insist that the family move a bit inland to Beaumont. Babe ran around in the lower-income, working-class neighborhood, playing sports all the time. She fought often against girls and boys, earning the nickname the "worst kind on Doucette Street."[4] She was adept with her hands in combat, protecting her siblings from other kids. At Beaumont High School, she starred on the school's golf, tennis, and basketball teams. The school's football coach even tried to recruit her to be his field goal kicker before school authorities foreclosed the possibility.

Basketball was her best sport, as she led her team to consecutive championships. Her hardwood exploits earned her the attention of Melvin J. McCombs, the coach of a Dallas-based semipro team called the Employer's Casualty Golden Cyclones. Women in those days competed in Industrial leagues. Employers would hire girls specifically to play on their sports teams. Officially Babe was hired as an office worker, but her real job was to help the Cyclones win basketball tournaments. McCombs persuaded Babe to leave school early to join the team. Babe left school in February 1930 and moved to Dallas.

Babe led the Cyclones to the 1931 AAU (American Athletic Union) championship in basketball. In the five games of the tournament, Babe averaged better than 20 points a game, an amazing feat given that in those teams some teams didn't score 20 points in an entire game. McCombs told a local Dallas newspaper: "Babe Didrikson was the easiest girl to coach and the hardest to handle of all the athletes I have had in the past fifteen years."[5]

Didrikson also competed in track and field events for the McCombs squad. Sometimes she was the entire squad. People sometimes talk about "one-man or one-woman teams." Usually that refers to one dominant player. Babe literally was a one-person team at times. In July 1930 she shattered the world records in the javelin toss and the baseball throw and finished second to the amazing Stella Walsh in the broad jump. Babe hurled a baseball 263 ft—10 ft more than the previous world record. Her efforts led Employers Casualty to a second-place finish to the Illinois Women's Athletic Association. The Illinois team scored 30 points, while Babe scored 19.

In July 1931, Babe again led Employers Casualty in the tenth annual national women's track and field championship. Babe won first place in the baseball throw, the broad jump, and the 80-m hurdles. She hurled the baseball 296 ft to shatter her own world record. Her closest competitor was more than 40 ft behind her. Unfortunately for the Babe and McCombs, the well-balanced Illinois Women's Athletic Club repeated as champions.[6] Illinois won in part because the AAU prohibited athletes from competing in more than three events—a rule that prevented Babe from defending her javelin throw title. "I think the A.A.U. ruling is powerful silly," the Babe told the United Press. "I just feel like throwing that old javelin out of the lot."[7] Before leaving the meet, Babe told reporters that her goal was to win several gold medals at the 1932 Olympic Games in Los Angeles.

Babe and McCombs smarted from the loss to the Illinois team and successfully petitioned the AAU to allow her to enter more events. The next year in July 1932 Babe was allowed to compete in more events. The result was arguably the most dominant one-day athletic performance in sports history. She won first place in five events—the javelin throw, the baseball toss, the shot put, the 80-m hurdles, and the broad jump. She added a fourth place finish in the discus. She failed to qualify in only the 50-m dash. Her amazing efforts earned "her team"—herself—first place with 30 points. The two-time defending champion Illinois squad had to settle for second with 22 points. "I came out here to beat everyone in sight in the high jump, the hurdles and the javelin throw," said the Babe. "America's greatest woman athlete? Well, that's what they call me."[8]

Her legendary performance also earned her the coveted trip to Los Angeles. Much to the Babe's dismay, Olympic officials limited her to three events. The Babe told sportswriter Grantland Rice that she had once entered eleven events at a single meet and could not understand why she should be limited. "Why should I get tired? I'm young and strong and I could play one game or another all day long."[9]

Babe mentioned that after the Olympic Games she would tackle golf. She told sportswriter Rice that she had only recently taken up the game—a statement that was not true—but the Babe had a pattern of exaggerating and telling tall tales.

She achieved international glory at the 1932 Olympics by capturing gold and silver medals in several events. She won gold medals in the javelin and 80-m hurdles and added a silver medal in the broad jump. The *Los Angeles Times* wrote:

> While the greatest collection of bulky-muscled behemoths and iron-limbed luminaries the world has ever known struggled all afternoon in their futile efforts to crack world records, it remained for a mere slip of a girl from Texas to prove that the female of the species is not only more deadly than the male but also more reliable when it comes to shattering official standards. Mildred (Babe) Didrikson, 128 pounds of feminine dynamite, came through yesterday when all competitors of the so-called stronger sex failed in their world-record attempts.[10]

In her first javelin toss, she hurled the object more than 143 ft on her very first toss. Even the former world record holder, Germany's Ellen Braumuller was powerful to stop the express train from Texas.

She won the 80-m dash in under 12 seconds, establishing a world record. Fellow American Evelyn Hall finished a very close second. In fact, many felt that Hall may have hit the tape first and should have been awarded the gold medal. Babe, who had injured herself in her first javelin toss, added a silver medal in the high jump even though she jumped the same height as gold medalist Jean Shiley. Officials awarded Shiley the gold medal because the Babe had jumped headfirst—not the proper way to clear the bar. The ruling was bizarre because the Babe had not been warned that her method of jumping was against any rule. Grantland Rice wrote that "it was another of those queer rulings or decisions that have occurred far too often in these Games."[11] Even so, he added that the Babe "did more than her share in contributing to the greatest slaughter of world's records every known to sport."[12] In another column Rice gushed in praise: "World's records to Mildred Babe Tex Didrikson, the Texas thunderbolt, are merely playthings in a toy shop. She takes them in her stride, whether it calls for a brawny arm or a pair of flying feet or the coordination of a leap of a lean, lithe body."[13]

Turning to the Links

Shortly after her Herculean performance at the Olympic games, the Babe announced that she was tackling a new challenge—golf. She declared on August 11, 1932, that she would enter a national links tournament in Peabody, Massachusetts. She declared that "from now on I am going to forget about track and field events and play golf daily in order to be on my game for the national."[14]

She could not return to track and field even if she desired because the Amateur Athletic Union banned her for advertising a commercial product. Babe had appeared in an ad for a Dodge automobile. Babe practiced golf

with fervor but also returned to Employer's Casualty in Dallas to earn a
living. In 1933 she embarked on a basketball tour against all-male teams.
One time her team even played the Harlem Globetrotters—an interracial
matchup unusual for that day.[15] Babe also played a series of exhibitions
with baseball teams in the summer of 1934. She also boxed a few exhibitions. All this barnstorming kept her name in the public eye, but Babe
wanted a different, more competitive challenge. These other sports bordered
on publicity stunt sideshows. Babe wanted real competition. Cayleff wrote:
"Golf alone offered her a future as a legitimate, respected, wage-earning
athlete."[16]

She became mesmerized after watching the great Bobby Jones and his
picture-perfect swing. The sport also afforded Babe the chance to compete
against male players—to push herself even harder. She practiced relent-
lessly, even hitting 1,500 drives a day till her hands bled. She approached
her would-be coach Stan Kertes by walking up and bluntly stating: "I want
to be the greatest woman golfer in the world."[17]

Babe went on an exhibition tour with male golfing legend Gene Sarazen,
the winner of number major championships. On the 1935 tour, Babe played
doubles with Sarazen against other players, including the great, retired
British champion Joyce Wethered. Babe could not match Wethered's scores
but she proved competitive.

Babe's improvement showed dramatically when she entered the Texas
Woman's Championship in Houston, Texas. She faced snobbery and snide
remarks from some other elitist players, such as Peggy Chandler, who allegedly said: "We really don't need any truck drivers' daughters in our tournament."[18] Babe laughed last when she took home top honors by defeating
none other Chandler in the final match.

The *Washington Post* editorialized:

The scoffers, as scoffers do, have faded into limbo, but the brilliant Babe is on her
way, according to the experts. A few touches here and there in her golf, some steady
practice, a bit more competition, and it's but a matter of time before she's the
national feminine golf champion, they agreed last week, marveling at the girl to
whom all sports come easy.[19]

The USGA (United States Golf Association)—much like the AAU before
it—suspended Babe for 3 years because she had accepted money for commercial advertising. Babe had to turn professional and make money where
she could in the sport.

In 1938, she entered the Los Angeles Open—a tournament for male
amateurs and pros but without a rule barring women. Babe shot an 83 but
accomplished something far more—she met George Zaharias, the professional wrestler. Known as "the Crying Greek from Cripple Creek" or "the
Colorado Crooner" or "the Meanest Man," George and Babe became fast

friends. Both were extroverts with charisma. Perhaps Babe met someone who exceeded her own gifts for self-promotion in the professional wrestler. The two married in January 1939. George promoted Babe, setting up exhibition matches for her all over the country.

In 1940, the 29-year-old Babe won the Western Women's Open in Milwaukee and the Texas Women's Open—two events she was eligible for as a professional. Unfortunately for Babe, the best players in the world were amateurs and she was barred from competing against them.

Babe tried her hand at tennis, but this sport too was dominated by amateurs. Then, Babe turned to bowling where she regularly staring rolling more than 200s. She won the Women's Open in San Francisco in 1941. George landed her on a popular exhibition tour with amateur great Patty Berg. The two women played entertaining giants Bob Hope and Bing Crosby. The men were decent golfers but no match for the two best American female golfers. Hope joked: "There's only one thing wrong about Babe and myself. I hit the ball like a girl and she hits it like a man."[20]

Babe was eligible to play as an amateur again in 1943 but this was in the midst of World War II when sporting events were interrupted by much larger world concerns. Toward the end of the war, Babe was finally able to test herself against the best women golfers of the day. Cayleff explains that "once she rejoined the top players in 1945, Babe's style revolutionized women's golf."[21]

Her style was unique and not aligned perfectly with traditional golf etiquette. She talked regularly with folks in the gallery. If she was having a bad day, she might say: "Ah couldn't hit an elephant's ass with a bull fiddle today."[22] The Babe rubbed some of her competitors the wrong way at times with her bravado and braggadocio. She was known to inquire boldly of her competitors as to which one of them was gunning for second place. Fellow pro Helen Dettweiler said it best: "She thinks she's whole show, which, of course, she is."[23] "Babe made it pretty clear from the start that she was the star," Louise Suggs recalled in 1995 at a meeting of U.S. Women's Open champions. "According to her, the rest of us were spear carriers."[24]

Even though her antics offended some of her fellow competitors, they increased attention to the sport, which ultimately benefited all the players. She began to dominate the women's game, winning thirteen straight tournaments beginning in August 1946. She did not lose in 1946—something that will never happen again in the sport of golf.

In 1947, she did something perhaps even more special—she broke the British curse by becoming the first American to win the British Championship. In the final round, the Babe faced London's Jacqueline Gordon in the 36-hole match-play championship event. The two battled evenly in the 18-hole morning round. For the afternoon round, Babe dumped "some refined" clothes (a gray flannel shirt, wool sweater, and white blouse) for her favored blue corduroy slacks. "The pants did it," the Babe would say later, as she raced to a commanding lead. She won 5 of the first 6 holes in the afternoon round and coasted to a 5 and 4 victory.[25]

In the second hole of the afternoon round, the Babe outdrove Gordon by nearly 100 yards. She also holed some long putts. At the 14th hole, she sank a long putt to close out the match. The Associated Press reported: "That putt also ended the most concentrated display of expert golf by a woman this windswept course on the Firth of Forth—not far from the birthplace of the game—ever had seen."[26]

While at the event, a few older British ladies approached one of England's finest golfers, Mrs. A.M. Holm, saying that the Babe needed a serious dose of refinement. Rhonda Glenn writes that Holm responded coolly: "You are speaking of the finest woman golfer that has ever been seen."[27]

In 1947, Babe also made a decision that forever changed the direction of women's golf—she signed as her agent Fred Corcoran, who represented such sports luminaries as Sam Snead, Stan Musial, and Ted Williams. A former caddy, Corcoran's charm enabled him to become tournament manager for the PGA in 1937.

Corcoran convinced Babe to forfeit her amateur status by accepting $300,000 for a series of ten golf films. "I really hated to give up my amateur status I had worked so hard to regain, but that money looked too good," the Babe said.[28]

He lined up a deal for Babe in which she received $8,000 a year to promote Wilson Sporting Goods' golf clubs. She endorsed a variety of products from Weathervane sportswear to Timex watches to automobile batteries to cigarettes. She also charged a fee of $1,000 for exhibition matches.

But Babe still wanted to perform on a higher golf stage—to win money playing the game she so dearly loved. Cayleff writes: "Having so few playing opportunities was frustrating. Other excellent women golfers felt the same way; it was next to impossible for women golfers to earn a living from their sport."[29]

Corcoran also negotiated with L.B. Icely, the president of Wilson Sporting Goods, who believed that women should have a professional venue to showcase their talent—and his golf equipment. They named the organization the Ladies Professional Golf Association. Babe and twelve other women are considered the founders of the LPGA. Finally, the Babe could play professionally against many of the best players in the world.

Everyone, including Babe of course, knew that she was the main draw. She did not disappoint, as she dominated the tour. In 1949, she won a third of the prize money. The next year she won more than half of the tournaments, including all three majors—the U.S. Women's Open, the Titleholders Championship, and the Western Open. In 1951, she led the tour in money earned for the third consecutive year.

In February 1950, the Associated Press announced its Women Athlete of the Half-Century poll. Babe received 319 first-place votes and a total of

leaping over hurdles, throwing a baseball, throwing a javelin or hitting a baseball, the "Babe" set a standard of performance unequaled by any woman and doubtless, envied by many a man.

When she eventually turned her talents to the ancient game of golf, it was only to be expected that she would conquer the difficulties of a game which has exasperated more would-be experts than any other game in history. Many thousands of golfers, on both sides of the Atlantic, watched with astonishment as this champion of the "weaker" sex clouted a tee-shot farther than they had ever seen a woman propel a ball before.[41]

In 1975 famed sportswriter Jim Murray in his column "the Other Babe" said that the Babe "did more for women than the Equal Rights Amendment."[42]

In 2000, *Sports Illustrated* listed its top-100 female athletes of the century. The Babe finished second only to track and field heptathlon star Jackie Joyner Kersee. Elinor Nickerson in *Golf: A Women's History* writes: "There is little doubt that she was the finest woman athlete of the century."[43] In 2000, ESPN listed its top-100 athletes of all time—male or female. The top ten were: Michael Jordan, Babe Ruth, Muhammad Ali, Jim Brown, Wayne Gretsky, Jesse Owens, Jim Thorpe, Willie Mays, Jack Nicklaus, and Babe Didrikson.[44]

She was the only woman listed in the top ten. The next closest was tennis great Martina Navratilova at nineteen. No other female golfer even cracked the prestigious list. "She was the most outstanding female athlete of the 20th century because of her multisport excellence," said Cayleff in a personal interview. "There really is no one comparable to her."[45]

PATTY BERG

With her willingness to give her famous clinic every tournament week and to graciously agree to every request for interviews, speeches and other appearances for sponsors, she set the standard for making friends for our organization that has guided the players for over 56 years.

—Besty Rawls[46]

She was not only a great player but probably the greatest shot maker ever on the LPGA tour.

—Marilyn Smith[47]

Patty Berg, who won several women's titles and then turned professional, is one of the greatest competitors I have seen in women's golf.

—Byron Nelson[48]

Patricia Jane Berg stood only 5-foot-2, but looms large in the annals of golf history, as she holds her rightful place in the pantheon of great female golfers.

She won a record fifteen major championships and sixty professional titles. Born in 1918 in Minneapolis, Minnesota, Berg did not immediately turn to golf. As a youngster she loved figure skating and speed skating. She placed second in a national competition in speed skating. She loved all sports, even contact sports with boys. Her athletic prowess was shown by her ability to play football on a local youth team. She served as quarterback for the 50th Street Tigers. One of her teammates was future college hall-of-fame coach Bud Wilkinson, who led the Oklahoma Sooners to multiple national championships. Her love of football even interfered with her schoolwork. One day when a teacher was writing questions for a test on the blackboard, the teacher looked over at Patty's paper and saw strange markings all over the page. The strange markings were diagrammed football plays.[49]

Her parents dissuaded her from continuing in physical contact sports, so they introduced the talented Patricia to golf. She played this new sport at the age of thirteen, and the rest was history. She said her mother did not see much of a future for her daughter in football. However, her mother certainly proved prescient with regard to her daughter having a better chance in golf. Her father purchased her a secondhand pair of golf clubs and a membership at the Interlachen Country Club in Edina, Minnesota.[50]

Success was not immediate in the game of golf. In one of her very first tournaments, Patty entered the 1933 Minneapolis City Championship where she made a whoppingly poor score of 122. Patty vowed that she would not let that happen again, that she would commit herself fully to improving her game over the next year.[51]

She worked on her game religiously with Lester Bolstad, who was to remain her coach for the next 40 years. "All I did was think and talk about golf the whole year."[52] The year of dedication paid dividends, as Berg won the same city tournament the next year. "I never thought I would win," she told great golf writer Liz Kahn, "and when I realized what I'd done in 365 days, I thought I could go on to play the big amateur tournaments and maybe someday have a future in golf."[53] Her thoughts proved correct, as she ended up having a lifelong affair with golf as perhaps its finest female ambassador.

In 1935, Berg made it all the way to the finals of the U.S. Amateur Championship. In 1936, Berg made international news when she sparkled in a golf exhibition in Northwood, England, in charity foursome matches. Berg won both of her matches and played as well as anybody involved, including maybe even the vaunted Joyce Wethered. Her performance in the English exhibition earned her a place on the 1936 and 1938 Curtis Cup teams, neither of which lost to the British teams.

1938 may have been the finest year of golf displayed by any woman in history, as Patty won ten of the thirteen tournaments she entered, including the U.S. amateur championship.

Patty Berg captured the Associated Press' top honors as Woman Athlete of the Year in 1938 after she won numerous titles, including the national championship. In her 7 years as an amateur, she won nearly thirty championships. She was as equally successful in the professional ranks.

She turned pro in 1940—10 years before the formation of the LPGA. In 1941, she won the Western Open, the North Carolina Open, and the New York Invitational. In June 1941, Bing Cosby and Bob Hope challenged Babe Didrikson and Patty Berg to a charity-sponsored doubles challenge match. While Cosby and Hope garnered laughs, the two powerful women produced the golf shots. The *Los Angeles Times* reported that the gallery of 2,500 watched "the girls prove that the female of the human race is nothing to be laughed off, especially on a golf course."[54] Babe shot a 74, Berg shot a 79, and the men both shot in the 80s.

However, her career took a detour after a serious automobile accident in December 1941. Patty and fellow golf star Helen Dettweiler were traveling to Palestine, Texas, for a golf exhibition when they collided with another vehicle near Corsicana, Texas. Dettweiler escaped injury, but Patty suffered a fractured left kneecap and a lacerated jaw.[55] The Associated Press reported that she "will undoubtedly be out of competitive golf for some time."[56] Dr. D.B. Carrell, a Dallas-based bone specialist, said that Berg suffered a double compound fracture and that her career was not in jeopardy.[57]

Berg plunged herself into rehab. The *New York Times* ran a photo caption titled "Pulling for a Comeback," showing her at a Mobile, Alabama, gymnasium pulling her arms on a weight machine.[58]

Berg made a triumphant comeback in July 1943 by winning the Western Open, her first competitive event since her auto accident. Berg rallied from 3 holes down after the 30th hole to defeat Dorothy Kirty 1-up in the 36-hole finals match. She "showed the competitive tenacity and skill that have established her as the country's no. 1 woman golfer."[59] After the match, Berg announced that she would sign up for the Marines, women's reserve. On July 24, the Marines officially announced from a Chicago office that Berg had been accepted into the Marines reserves. The Marines trained her in Camp Lejune in North Carolina and then placed her in recruitment where her exuberant personality would shine. Arthur Daley of the *New York Times* wrote: "In her is the steel of which true Marines are made."[60]

Her dramatic comeback from injury culminating in her second Western Open title earned her Woman Athlete of the Year honors in 1943 from the Associated Press. She received 30 of a possible 52 first-place votes and outdistanced her nearest competitor 118 to 76.[61]

For the next 2 years Berg did not participate in tournament play. She practiced only twice a week because of her Marine duties as a lieutenant. She called the experience wonderful and one she would "never forget." In September 1945, she was placed on inactive duty and looked forward to returning to golf full time. "I'm going to take a rest and I'm going to take some lessons from my teacher, Lester Bolstad."[62]

Berg won the first Women's Open Championship in 1946—a match-play competition in Spokane, Washington—by besting Betty Jameson in the finals by a score of 5 and 4. The grand prize was a record $5,600.

Throughout her long career, which lasted until 1980, Berg showed remarkable poise down the stretch. In the 1948 Western Open Golf championship, she rallied from four strokes down in the last 6 holes over Babe Didrikson to win in a sudden-death play-off. Berg's exploits were all the more remarkable given that she dealt with a left-hand sprain for much of the tournament.[63] 1948 was a banner year for Berg, as she won seven titles.

She played a key role in the formation of the LPGA with the Babe in 1949–50. She served as the LPGA's first president. The next year in 1951, Berg, the Babe, Jameson, and Louise Suggs were inducted into the LPGA Hall of Fame.

She faced down the dominant Babe again at the 1951 Weathervane Cross-Country Golf Tournament in Great Neck, New York. Tied after regulation, the two rivals engaged in a dramatic 36-hole play-off. In the second day of overtime, Berg shot a 75 to Babe's 76 to earn another close victory over her chief nemesis.

In 1952, Berg set a world record by firing a 64 at the Richmond, California, country club in the Richmond Ladies PGA Open golf tournament. Par was 74, but Berg proved magical with her putter. During her round, she carded ten birdies and only one bogey. Berg's 64 bested by two strokes the previous record of 66 shared by Mrs. Opal Hill, Babe Didrikson Zaharias, and Grace Lenczik.

In 1955, Berg led the tour in money earned with a total of $16,492.34 and also captured the Vardon trophy for the player with the lowest average scoring in championship play. Her efforts enabled her to win the 1955 Associated Press award for best female athlete, defeating the Babe by a vote of 200 to 146.[64]

Some of her fellow pros believed that Berg was actually the better player. Betty Hicks was quoted in the *Washington Post:* "measured by the yardstick of tournaments won, Patty Berg is a better golfer than Mrs. Zaharias. As the pros who is our greatest shot maker. We'll tell you it's Patty Berg."[65] Mickey Wright once said that "Babe Zaharias couldn't carry Patty Berg's golf clubs."[66]

Rhonda Glenn, manager of communications for the USGA and author of *The Illustrated History of Women's Golf,* said Berg should be considered one of the five greatest players in the history of the game. "She simply dominated amateur golf during her era, winning 27 amateur championships and, of course, went on to a magnificent professional career, winning a record 15 major championships. She was also a medalist in most of her amateur tournaments."

"In looking at her game, Patty had all the shots: she was a great driver of the ball, iron player, short game, one of the best bunker players of all time, and a wonderful putter," Glenn says. "She had the added qualities of being able to think her way around a golf course and was a strong performer under pressure. Those qualities made her a great golfer."[67]

Even as she advanced in age, she still retained her formidable game. In 1959, Patty sank the first hole-in-one during LPGA tournament play at the U.S. Women's Open in Churchill Valley Country Club in Pittsburgh.

"She carried the name of Wilson and the LPGA into every corner of the golfing world," said Betsy Rawls. "People came to see her time after time, always laughing at the jokes, always admiring the crisp shots, and always loving Patty Berg."[68]

Berg died in September 2006 at the age of eighty-eight.

LOUISE SUGGS

In June 1946, the leading women golfers of the day descended upon Des Moines, Iowa, for the prestigious Western Open. The event featured two perennial favorites—two-time defending champion Babe Didrikson and Patty Berg, winner of the title in 1941 and 1943. The golfing experts predicted a typical Babe vs. Berg final. However, a young 22-year-old from Georgia had other ideas. Her name was Louise Suggs.

Suggs defeated the mighty Babe 1-up in the semifinals with her "courageous play."[69] Her superior putting carried her to the narrow victory. Then, she "climaxed one of the most thrilling weeks in the history of women's golf" by defeating Berg 2-up in the 36-hole final.[70] Berg complimented her young rival: "Louise is a great golfer," Berg said. "She deserved to win. You'll hear a lot from her for a long time."[71]

Berg was right, as the golfing world heard much from Louise Suggs for a long time. Like the Babe and Berg, Suggs was one of the founding members of the LPGA and one of the greatest players in the history of the game. Standing only 5-foot-2 and weighing only 112 pounds in her prime, Suggs loomed as one of the sport's great giants. Her prowess on the links earned her the nickname Lithia Springs Louise from the press for her hometown and "Louise Sluggs" from comedian Bob Hope for her ability to hit long drives off the tee. Some even referred to her as the female Ben Hogan because of her intense concentration, focus, and pure swing.

Born in Atlanta, Georgia, in 1923, Suggs learned the game at the age of ten from her father, a former baseball player who retired to run a golf course. She ended up winning eleven majors and fifty-eight LPGA events in her illustrious career.

At sixteen, she upset Mrs. Marion Miley to advance in the 1940 Augusta women's invitational golf tournament. In January 1941, the 17-year-old Georgia state champion served notice she was a national force when she won the Charlotte Harbor golf tournament in Punta Gorda, Florida, with a final-round victory over Elizabeth Hicks by a score of 3 and 2. In May

1941, she defeated Mrs. Don Chandler 7 and 6 in the Southern Open final held in Memphis, Tennessee. In March 1942, the Associated Press referred to her as a "rising star among golfers."[72]

1946 was a banner year for Suggs, as she won numerous titles, including her aforementioned Western Open title where she beat the Babe and the Berg in successive days. Later that year, she stopped the improbable run of Mary McMillan, the "Cinderella girl" who had upset the Babe in the semifinals of the Western amateur title in Cleveland, Ohio. Suggs dominated the final, winning by a lopsided score of 11 and 10. McMillan said afterward: "I got a beating, but gosh it sure was fun. My Irish luck just didn't hold out."[73]

Suggs retained her Western Open title in June 1947 with a 4 and 2 victory over Mrs. Dorothy Kirby. In 1948, she led the U.S. Curtis Cup squad to a victory over the British team. Less than 2 weeks later she became the second American (after the Babe in 1947) to win the British Women's Amateur tournament with a dramatic 1-up victory on the 36th and final hole over Scotland's Jean Donald in a sloggy environment.

In July 1948 she announced she was turning professional as an advisor for MacGregor golf equipment. Later that year in a highly publicized duel, the three-woman team of Suggs, Dot Kielty, and Dot Kirby defeated comedian Bob Hope and Johnny Dawson in an exhibition match.[74]

In 1949, she won the Western Open for a third time by defeating Betty Jameson 5 and 4. Later that year in September she routed her competitors to win the Women' U.S. Open. Her next closest competitor was Babe Zaharias who finished fourteen strokes behind. Her four-round total was 291, while the Babe came in second with 305 and Patty Berg a distant third at 310. Actor James Dunn, who won an Oscar for the movie *A Tree Grows in Brooklyn,* presented Louise with the winner's check of $1,500.[75]

She added a second U.S. Open crowd in 1952 by setting a world-record 72-hole score of 284 at the Bala Golf Club in Philadelphia, Pennsylvania. She fired successive rounds of 70, 69, 70, and 75 to win by seven shots over Marlene Bauer and Betty Jameson. She earned $1,750 for her first-place victory.[76] She claimed that she had no idea that she was besting the Babe's previous record of 288. "I wasn't thinking of any record on the last few holes," she said. "In fact, at the seventeenth hole, I handed my driver to a marshal. I was concentrating so hard that I mistook him for my caddy."[77]

In 1953, she led the LPGA tour in money earned. She won consecutive tournaments in San Diego and then in Bakersfield, California, with a sudden-death victory over Patty Berg. In June of that year, she won the Weathervane Cross-Country Golf tournament by eleven strokes. The unique 144-hole event required the players to play at several golf courses—eight rounds of golf. Suggs carded a 593, while the second-place Berg posted a 604.[78] She capped off perhaps her finest year as a professional by winning her fourth Western Open crown with a final-round win over Patty Berg 6 and 5.

In 1954, she won the Titleholders championship with another convincing victory—seven strokes. In Spartanburg, South Carolina, she sank a 24-ft putt on the first play-off hole to defeat Marlene Bauer at the Peach Classic-Betsy Rawls tournament. The next month she won the Babe Zaharias Open over none other than the Babe by two strokes.

In 1955, Suggs rallied from seven strokes behind in the final round to win the Eastern Open title by a single stroke over Faye Crocker of Montevideo, Uruguay. Suggs carded a final-round 69 to take the title.

She added three more major championships with the 1956 Titleholders, the 1957 LPGA Championship, and the 1959 Titleholders titles. She won her last major at the 1959 Titleholders with a narrow one-stroke victory over Betsy Rawls. She nearly added another major title in the 1959 U.S. Women's Open but lost by two strokes to the dominant Mickey Wright.

In 1961, Suggs won the Palm Beach Invitational, a unique par-3 tournament featuring top men and women professionals. Suggs, who had claimed that women could beat men on short courses, proved her point at this tournament where she beat twelve male professionals, including Sam Snead, two-time Masters champion Henry Picard, former U.S. Open champion Lew Worsham, Clyde Usina, and former PGA champion Chick Herbert. The woman nicknamed "Little Miss Poison" proved too much to handle for the men. Suggs fired a three-round score of 156—one better than Dub Pagan and two better than the legendary Snead.[79]

Suggs—along with the Babe, Patty Berg, and Betty Jameson—was elected to the LPGA Hall of Fame in 1951. In 1979, she was inducted into the World Golf Hall of Fame. In her illustrious career, she won fifty-eight career titles, including eleven major championships.

— CHAPTER 5 —

FORMING THE LPGA AND OTHER GREATS OF THAT ERA

I never thought of myself as a pioneer. We were just a bunch of stubborn women who loved golf and figured we could make it happen.

—Marlene Bauer Hagge, one of the LPGA original founding players[1]

Up until 1940, the best lady golfers were amateur golfers. The great British player Joyce Wethered had dominated international golf as an amateur. Her friendly American rival Glenna Collett Vare did the same on American shores. The picture began to change in 1940, as more women desired to make money off their athletic exploits.

L.B. Icely, the head of Wilson Sporting Goods, signed several young women to contracts to promote Wilson golfing products. Wilson was a pioneer in woman's golf and had designed clubs specifically for women since 1927. Icely signed Helen Hicks in 1934, Opal Hill in 1938, Helen Dettweiler in 1939, and Patty Berg in 1940. The women played exhibitions, showcased products, and held clinics.

A group of women, including Hicks and Berg, discussed the idea of forming their own professional league. In December 1944, they helped form the WPGA (Women's Professional Golf Association) with 1941 U.S. amateur champion Betty Hicks as president, Ellen Griffin as vice president, and Hope Segnious as secretary and treasurer. When forming the WPGA, the women invalidated two racially discriminatory provisions that would have prohibited nonwhites from playing on the tour.[2] Hicks campaigned hard for the removal of the offending clauses in part because they would have prohibited her Chinese-American friend Jackie Pung from playing on tour.

Hope Segnious kept the tour alive with financial aid from her father. She published a golf magazine to promote the tour and organized a Women's Open Championship. However, the tour failed to get off the ground successfully. "Hope thought it would be a good idea to get some girls together and try to get golf started on a pro basis," Helen Dettweiler told Rhonda Glenn for her *The Illustrated History of Women's Golf.* "She had a lot of great ideas but they were, unfortunately, much too early."[3]

When Segnious resigned, Icely contacted sports agent Fred Corcoran, a former PGA tournament director, and asked him to oversee the development of a women's tour. In his book *Unplayable Lies,* Corcoran relates that Icely contacted him, saying: "If I can get the other manufacturers to come in, will you set up a woman's tour?"[4]

Corcoran, Patty Berg, and Babe and her husband George Zaharias met at the Venetian Hotel in Miami, Florida, to discuss a new women's professional league. "I think you have to give a lot of credit to Hope Segnious, and her dad, because they helped us a lot," Patty Berg told Glenn in her *The Illustrated History of Women's Golf.* "She had tremendous vision, but I thought that we just had to get going, that's all. We had to get somebody with Fred's background."[5]

The first order of business was to see if they could obtain the charter from the failing WPGA. The WPGA resigned in part because they had put a lot of money into a golfing magazine. Corcoran said that he then contacted his lawyer from New York who told him to change the name to "Ladies."[6] The other version for the name selection was that Corcoran convinced the group to change the name to Ladies Professional Golf Association— the LPGA—because, as Patty Berg said, "He thought 'Ladies' sounded nicer."[7]

"The announcement that we had formed the Ladies' PGA touched off a national storm of indifference," Corcoran wrote. "Potential sponsors were polite when I called them, but you could hear them sifting a yawn at the other end of the phone."[8]

Corcoran obtained assistance from Weathervane Sports Clothes Company, which put forth the prize money for the tour events. Alvin Handmacher, the head of Weathervane, eventually became convinced that his company could profit by having the women professional players using his company's products. "I wouldn't go so far as to say that, without Alvin Handmacher and his Weathervane championships, there wouldn't be a woman's pro tour today," Corcoran wrote. "But let's make no mistake about it. Alvin put the Ladies PGA in business....Today the girls are playing for a quarter of a million dollars [in 1965]—and it was Handmacher who cracked the safe."[9] Corcoran also credits Helen Lengfeld, a woman from California and a lover of women's golf, who published the *National Golfer* magazine. She built a Pacific Coast tour for the women that greatly helped the LPGA in its infancy.

But Corcoran himself played a major role in women's golf. It is for this reason that he was inducted into the World Golf Hall of Fame. "Fred Corcoran was a huge booster for women's golf," says Susan Cayleff. "He promoted Babe's career and was very instrumental in bringing in early sponsors."[10] Corcoran did whatever he could to drum up publicity for the LPGA, even suggesting mixed-gender matches. In 1952, Corcoran, one of the founders of the LPGA, said the current lady professional players could top many male amateurs. He specifically tried to promote a match between the Babe and U.S. male amateur champ Billy Maxwell. "The Babe, for instance, has had 64s on championship courses," he told the *Washington Post.* "I have heard a lot of leading amateur players say they want no match with her."[11] He said the "Big Four of Women's Golf"—Babe, Berg, Louise Suggs, and Betty Jameson—could compete for a U.S. men's amateur title.

The new group elected Berg as President, Dettweiler as vice president, Jameson as treasurer, and Sally Sessions as treasurer. The LPGA consisted of thirteen founding players: Alice Bauer, Patty Berg, Bettye Danoff, Helen Dettweiler, Marlene Bauer Hagge, Helen Hicks, Opal Hill, Betty Jameson, Sally Sessions, Marilyn Smith, Shirley Spork, Louise Suggs, and Babe Zaharias.

In 2000, Spork recalled her decision to turn pro. She was having breakfast with Babe and her husband George when the Babe asked her if she was going to go pro. Spork responded, "How do you turn pro?" The Babe stood up and hit her on the head and said, "Kid now you're a pro."[12]

The financial rewards were often nonexistent in the beginning. The dedication to the sport and the LPGA was very much a "labor of love" for these thirteen women. They barnstormed the country, working hard to promote the infant league. They suffered through subpar playing conditions, low pay, and meager crowds. To save money they shared rooms in one-star hotels and traveled together in automobiles. But they persevered, and because of their perseverance, players like Annika Sorenstam can make more than $1 million in a single season.

"I think it's terrific," Berg said. "When you first start something, you never know how it's going to turn out. But I think the Ladies Professional Golf Association is the greatest women's professional sports organization in the world today. It's getting bigger and bigger, better and better and greater and greater."[13]

But in those days the tour struggled at times. The ladies had to play a transcontinental tournament, or progressive tournament, sponsored by the Weathervane Company where they literally would play at four different courses across the country.

The tour gained more legitimacy once the public saw the quality of the ladies' golfing, which was substantial. Corcoran gathered a group of the LPGA girls and took them to England in 1951 where they trounced a group of top British players. On the trip, the Babe defeated Leonard Crawley, a former British Walker Cup Player of some note and a golfing writer. When the two met on the course, Crawley patronizingly asked if Babe was going to tee off from the red tees—the shorter women's tees. "Ah'm playin' with you, son," the Babe replied. She proceeded to destroy Crawley.[14]

The Babe's charismatic personality carried the tour in those early days. Corcoran recalled:

If Alvin Handmacher made the women's tour possible, it was Babe Zaharias who made it go. She was the color, the gate attraction. She was, without doubt, the greatest woman athlete the world has ever seen—and probably the greatest woman golfer of all time, although I'd rank Glenna Collett Vare right up there with her, and Joyce Wethered of England, Louise Suggs and Patty Berg a half-step behind them.[15]

There were other great players in the early years of the LPGA besides the great Babe Zaharias, Patty Berg, and Louise Suggs. Three others were Betty Jameson, Betsy Rawls, and Marlene Bauer Hagge.

BETTY JAMESON

Betty Jameson was called golf's "first glamour girl." She captured majors before and after the formation of the LPGA. She was also known as one of the "Big Four" with the Babe, Berg, and Suggs. She won the Women's Western Open in 1942 and 1954. She also captured the U.S. Women's Open in 1947. She was born in Norman, Oklahoma, in 1919; her family moved to San Antonio, Texas, when she was very young. It was in Texas that she displayed the strokes that would take her near the top of women's professional golf.

She won the Texas Publinx at thirteen and then the state championship. At fifteen, she added the Texas Women's Amateur. Jameson was known as a very classy player and individual. She displayed that class when in 1952 she donated a trophy to the LPGA under the name of her idol, Glenna Collett Vare. The Vare Trophy is presented to the LPGA tour player with the lowest scoring average.

In 2005, the LPGA honored Jameson with the so-called Jameson Classic Pro-Am, organized by Sandra Ericksson, Judy Dickinson, and Robin Bernstein. "It's a wonderful recognition," said Jameson, who resides in Delray Beach, Florida, in 2006 on the eve of the second annual Jameson Classic. "It's unbelievable the feeling I have. I'm just joyful, grateful."[16]

BETSY RAWLS

Amazingly, Betsy Rawls did not pick up a golf club until she was seventeen. She learned quickly, winning the Texas Amateur 4 years later at twenty-one. She graduated Phi Beta Kappa from the University of Texas and then obtained her postgraduation working on the LPGA tour, learning from competing with the likes of Babe Zaharias, Patty Berg, Louise Suggs, and Betty Jameson.

She won eight major championships: the U.S. Women's Open four times in 1951, 1953, 1957, and 1960; the Women's Western Open in 1952 and 1959; and the LPGA Championship in 1959 and 1969. She won forty-seven other LPGA tournaments in a career that lasted until 1975. She won the GAC Classic in 1972 at forty-four, years beyond her prime.

She was the tour's leader in tournament wins in 1952, 1957, and 1959. Her best year was 1959 when she won ten tournaments, including two major championships.

As great a golfer as Rawls was—and she was great—she accomplished perhaps even more after her playing career was finished. She served 6 years as the LPGA's tournament director and then executive director of the McDonald's Championships—a marquis event on the tour. "She is such a jewel," said Kathy Whitworth. "If there's a controversy or a problem or a decision that has to be made on which direction they're going to go, she just has this wonderful way about her of picking things apart and looking at it from every angle. She's so smart."[17]

Rawls was inducted into the LPGA Hall of Fame in 1960 and in 1980 became the first woman to officiate in the men's U.S. Open. Rawls was a pioneer and a true professional who has given much to the game of women's golf and golf in general.

MARLENE BAUER HAGGE

Marlene Bauer Hagge set a record in 1950 that still stands today and may stand for ever given current LPGA rules: she joined the tour at age fifteen (a few weeks before she turned sixteen). She began playing golf at the age of three, as her father, Dave Bauer, leased a city golf course in Aberdeen, South Dakota. Mr. Bauer moved his family to the golf course, and so Marlene and her sister Alice were literally reared on golf.

She won the Los Angeles Open at thirteen when there was a sign on the course that read: "Children Under 14 Are Not Allowed."[18] She and her sister were original founding players of the LPGA. In 1952, Marlene won her first LPGA tournament, the Sarasota Open, at the age of eighteen. She remains the youngest woman to ever win an LPGA tournament. Standing 5-foot-2 and 110 pounds, Marlene attracted attention for her stunning good looks.

She won twenty-six LPGA tournaments, including the 1956 U.S. Open Championship in a play-off win over the great Patty Berg. She won her last championship 20 years after her first in 1972 at the Burdine's Invitational tournament.

MARILYN SMITH

Marilyn Smith won twenty-one LPGA tournaments, including back-to-back major championships at the Titleholders Championship in 1963 and 1964. Smith was one of the original founding members of the LPGA who helped pave the way for later generations of players. She won the NCAA Championship in 1949 and then joined the LPGA in its infancy the next year. She served as the LPGA's secretary in 1957 and as its president from 1958 to 1960. She later served as the first female television commentator at men's pro golf events.[19]

CHAPTER 6

THE TWO GREATEST WINNERS: MICKEY WRIGHT AND KATHY WHITWORTH

Heading into the 1960s, the game of women's golf had some of its greatest and personable stars. The "Big Four" of the Babe, Patty Berg, Louise Suggs, and Betty Jameson had carried the LPGA tour in those beginning years through most of the 1950s. Betsy Rawls dominated the late 1950s and began to pile up victories at an amazing pace. But new stars were emerging. The late 1950s and especially the 1960s would usher into the sporting world two young women who would become the game's two greatest tournament winners: Mickey Wright and Kathy Whitworth. Wright won eighty-two career tournaments, while Whitworth surpassed this record with eighty-eight victories.

MICKEY WRIGHT

> When Wright was over a shot, it was a dictatorship. Her opponents remember: Equal parts satin and steel, that's what her golf swing was, as pretty as it was powerful. They remember the sound of club meeting ball, loud and crisp, like it was amplified. They remember the flight of her shots, high and soaring, so different from every other woman. When someone told Wright she hit it like a man, she smiled.
>
> —Bill Fields[1]

Many golfing experts consider Mickey Wright to be the greatest golfer on the distaff side in the history of the game. She won eighty-two professional golf tournaments even though she retired at the young age of thirty-four in 1969. She won twelve major championships in a span of 8 years. "I always say Mickey was the best golfer the LPGA ever had," said fellow Hall of Famer Betsy Rawls. "I think most of the people who ever saw her play still think that. She sort of revolutionized golf for us because she was so good and her swing was so perfect. Even though we were competitors, she was a joy to watch."[2] Ben Hogan said that Wright had the best golf swing he had ever seen.

Like most great golfers, apart from incredible Babe, Wright began winning tournaments as a junior player. Reared in San Diego, her father Arthur Wright, a lawyer, bought her a set of clubs when she was young. "It was a real cheap set," she said years later. "There were four clubs—a wood, two irons and a putter. The very first day I broke all four swinging at the ball. That convinced my father I had enough power to hit the ball."[3] Her parents had divorced since she was three, but Wright found an outlet for her energies—golf. It became nearly an obsession. "I wanted to be the best woman golfer in the world," she said, "and that was from age 10 on."[4]

In July 1949 she won the Southern California Junior Girls' Golf Championship by defeating a girl named Barbara Hunter 5 and 4. In 1952, she won the National Junior Golf title by defeating Barbara McIntyre on the 18th hole. Wright sank a crucial putt that her opponent missed—a pattern that would surface repeatedly throughout her professional career.

Wright possessed the single-minded focus, determination, and discipline necessary to become an all-time great, in addition, of course, to excellent athletic ability. She realized early on that prior preparation prevents poor performance. When she was thirteen she had the idea that she wanted to be the best ever. She earned all-American honors as a student at Stanford University.

The larger public took notice of Wright at the 1954 National Open Golf Championship. Wright competed as an amateur against the legends of the game, including the Babe and Berg. The tournament belonged to the Babe, who won the championship in a runaway fashion by twelve strokes. However, Mickey Wright served notice that she would be heard from again, as she played with the Babe in the final two rounds, carding a 79 and a final-round 76. The *Los Angeles Times* reported that "she made a hit" with everyone who saw her, including the Babe, who remarked: "She's a real comer."[5] Later in the year, Wright fell to Barbara Romack in the finals of the Women's Amateur National Championship.

She joined the LPGA tour in 1955 but did not hit the winner's circle until the next year. At the age of twenty-one in 1956, she publicly announced her childhood goal. What was different about the young woman the press called "Pretty Mickey" was that she recognized that it would take incredible discipline and practice to reach such a lofty goal. "I'll have to work harder, much harder than anyone else," she said. "I've set up a definite training schedule for myself—9 or 10 hours a sleep every night, a couple of hours practice every morning and another hour after my round."

In her sophomore season, Wright won her first LPGA event at the 1956 Jacksonville Open with a tremendous rally. Trailing by three shots with 8 holes remaining, Wright overtook Joyce Ziske. Wright had defeated the likes of Patty Berg, Louise Suggs, and Betsy Rawls—truly great players.

Wright won her first Women's Open Championship in 1958 at the age of twenty-three. Her 2-under par total placed her five strokes ahead of second-place finisher Louise Suggs. Earlier in the year, Wright also had won the LPGA Championship, making her the first competitor to win both major titles in the same year. Wright successfully defended her title in 1959 with a two-stroke victory over Suggs.

In 1961, Wright won three of the four LPGA major tournaments—the U.S. Women's Open, the LPGA Championship, and the Titleholders Championship.

Wright won her third Open title after a second-round of 80. Wright rallied with a third-round 69 and a final round of 72 to capture the title by six strokes over Betsy Rawls. She followed that with a one-stroke victory over legends Patty Berg and Louise Suggs at the Titleholders Championship.

In 1963, Wright may have been at her peak, as she won a whopping thirteen tournaments, earned a then record $34,000 in prize money and captured the Vare Trophy for low scoring average. Her exploits that year won her the prestigious Associated Press Women Athlete of the Year award, outdistancing tennis great Maria Bueno by a vote of 311 to 127. The Associated Press noted that writers were supposed to vote for first, second, and third place women athletes, but that "many of them stopped after writing 'Mickey Wright.'"[6]

She followed an amazing 1963 with another great year in 1964. She won her fourth Open crown that year with an 18-hole play-off victory over Ruth Jessen. Wright showed her grit in the clutch, making a saving par from the bunker on the last hole of regulation to even force a play-off. From there she coolly captured the title by firing a 70.

Wright finished with eighty-two victories, a mark later broken by Kathy Whitworth who won eighty-eight. Even Whitworth acknowledges that Wright could have put her record beyond reach if she had not decided to retire early. "If not for a career decision by Mickey Wright, my total never would have set a record," she said. "Mickey was the best I've ever seen, without a doubt. She retired earlier than she had to, and if she'd kept going she surely would have won more than the 82 she had when she quit for good. Just playing regularly, she easily could have surpassed 100."[7]

Whitworth may well have been right, as Wright won eighty tournaments by the age of thirty-three. She was on pace to easily win more than 100. Whatever the case, Mickey Wright indeed had "the right stuff." Her all-time greatness is recognized by her peers in the golfing world. In 2000 *Golf Digest* brought together three great champions: Louise Suggs, JoAnne Carner, and Dottie Pepper. When asked who the greatest player of all time was, all three had the same answered "Mickey Wright."[8]

KATHY WHITWORTH

If one envisioned the all-time winner in professional golf history, one would not expect that golfer to have first swung a golf club at the age of fifteen. A more realistic picture would be of a young infant force-fed the sport since she were a toddler—someone groomed since birth to be a world champion. However, the all-time leading tournament winner in professional golf history—male or female—is Kathy Whitworth. In a professional career that spanned parts of five decades, Whitworth set new levels of consistent excellence that may never be broken.

From 1966 to 1973, Whitworth dominated her sport. She won LPGA Player of the Year honors seven times: 1966, 1967, 1968, 1969, 1971, 1972, and 1973. She won the Vare Trophy (for lowest scoring average) seven times.

Born in New Mexico in September 1938, Whitworth did not look the part of a future world-class athlete. She weighed 215 pounds in eighth grade. At age fifteen, she discovered a golf course and the rest was history. She learned the game quickly, winning the New Mexico State Amateur title in 1957 and 1958. The next year she turned professional.

Today we hear the importance of fitness for athletes. Whitworth proved this true, as she reduced her weight to 170 pounds in 1959 (her rookie year on the tour) and got down to 145 pounds in 1962—the year she won her first LPGA tournament. It took Whitworth some time before she started winning. Her first tournament win—at the Kelly Girls Open—was the seventy-ninth tournament of her PGA career. She won a tournament for seventeen consecutive years from 1962 to 1978.

Of her amazing winning, Whitworth wrote for *Golf Digest:* "I started out trying to win one tournament. Then I wanted to win a second to prove the first one wasn't a fluke. Then I thought, maybe I can keep doing this. The next thing I knew, I had 88."[9]

Whitworth's first major run occurred in the late 1960s, when she consistently won numerous tournaments. She won eight tournaments in 1965, eight tournaments in 1966, nine tournaments in 1967, ten tournaments in 1968, and seven tournaments in 1969. She had a rebirth in 1974, a year in which she captured seven tournaments. At times she ran away with golf tournaments, far outpacing the competition. In November 1965, she won the Titleholders Golf Championship by ten shots over Peggy Wilson. Her performance garnered her Associated Press Athlete of the Year honors. She garnered 101 first-place votes and a total of 441 points, outpacing Australian player Margaret Smith by more than 200 points.[10] She won the coveted Associated Press award for a second time in 1966, garnering 185 first-place votes for a total of 729 points—200 points more than the tennis great Billie Jean King.[11]

In 1979 and 1980, Whitworth did not win a single tournament—an unusual event, given that she had won at least one tournament the previous

17 years. Some speculated that the decline was imminent—that she would not win any more tournaments. She was only thirtieth on the money list in 1979 and twenty-fourth in 1980. The question persisted whether she at 40 years plus could rebound. "I was really depressed about my game during that time," she said in 1982. "I knew I didn't want to continue if I couldn't play top-notch golf. But I never really thought I was over the hill. Others did, though, I know, because a lot of the players stopped saying hi to me."[12]

She went back to her old coach, the legendary Harvey Penick, for advice and tutelage. He instilled in Whitworth a renewed faith in her swing and she rebounded. She put those doubts to rest and gave chase to Mickey Wright (eighty-two) and Sam Snead (eighty-four) for all-time wins.

In April 1982, Whitworth tied Mickey Wright with her eighty-second win at the women's International Golf Tournament at Hilton Head Island in South Carolina. She dominated the field that tournament, shooting a second-round 68 and a final-round 67 to win the tournament by nine strokes. "I feel like when I get it going, I swing as good as I ever did," she said after the eighty-second win.[13] She certainly earned the respect of second-year player and second-place finisher Patty Sheehan (who would go on to a Hall of Fame career in her own right): "It was like she was playing in another tournament, and I was the leader of everybody else. The only way anybody was going to catch her was if she completely fell apart, and she wasn't going to do that. She was awesome out there today."[14]

In early May 1982, Whitworth had a chance to break Mickey Wright's hallowed record at the United Virginia Bank Classic. In the final round, Whitworth shot a respectable 71, but was tied by Sally Litte's amazing 67. The two went into sudden death, and Little birdied the play-off hole for the victory. However, later in May, Whitworth won the Lady Michelob title in Atlanta, Georgia, for her eighty-third title, breaking Wright's LPGA record. After the event she said: "Winning a number of tournaments has never been a major goal for me. I guess it just means that I've been able to play a long time."[15] Donna Caponi, a great LPGA player in her own right, presented Kathy with a bouquet of roses after the historic win. In the clubhouse, she received a congratulatory note from none other than Mickey Wright: "Let everyone else worry about the 82d-83d wins. You just worry about No. 100."[16]

"Mr. Stats" Elliot Kalb writes of Whitworth well in his book *Who's Better, Who's Best in Golf:* "She won more than anyone else in the past and even Tiger Woods might not reach 88 wins in the future."[17]

The Two Best?

Most experts agree that Mickey Wright and Kathy Whitworth rank among the top-five women golfers of all time. Their inclusion is merited by the sheer number of tournament wins. They proved their greatness years later when Whitworth was forty-six and Wright fifty. They entered into the PGA's Legends of Golf Tournament, competing against senior golf greats such as Sam Snead, Don January, and Billy Casper. They fired a first-round 65, probably putting quite a scare in their male competitors. They finished a respectable nineteenth place out of twenty-eight teams. The *New York Times* wrote: "Despite a failure to contend for the title, Miss Whitworth and Miss Wright have shown they can play professionally with these senior male professionals."[18] This apparently caused an uproar as, later that year, another seniors tournament sought assurances from the PGA tour commissioner that the event would be for men only. The stated reason was that it was not fair to allow Whitworth, who was only forty-six, to enter the tournament field when everyone else was at least 50 years.[19] Perhaps another reason was a fear that these two women greats would have been a little too competitive. In either event, there is no disputing that Mickey Wright and Kathy Whitworth were two of the greatest golfers—and winners—to ever play the game.

OTHER GREATS IN THE 1960s AND 1970s

Carol Mann

Mickey Wright and Kathy Whitworth were the dominant golfers of their time but for the late 1960s they were seriously challenged—and often beaten—by another female golfer by the name of Carol Mann. Standing 6-foot-3, she towered over her opponents literally and figuratively from 1965 to 1975.

The *Chicago Daily Tribune* once referred to a 17-year-old Mann as "6 Feet 1½ Inches of Title Timber."[20] Mann's tall frame enabled her to drive the ball much further than her more diminutive opponents. For example, she captured the Women's Western Golf Association juniors championship over Sharon Fladoos by overpowering her younger opponent off the tee.

She began slowly on the pro tour after she joined in 1961, not winning a tournament until 1964. But she sure picked a big one, as her first professional title was the 1964 Women's Western Open Invitational. She followed that with the 1965 Women's Open—her second major.

While she failed to win another major championship in her career, she put together some dominant seasons. She won four tournaments in 1966, three tournaments in 1967, ten tournaments in 1968, and eight tournaments in 1969.

She continued to win tournaments in the 1970s, winning four tournaments in 1975 alone. She served as the LPGA's president from 1973 to 1976—a time during which the tour made the apt decision to hire Ray Volpe as commissioner.

Mann continued to have a great impact on the game as a popular golf announcer.

Judy Rankin

Another top golfer emerged in the late 1960s. This woman became a force in the 1970s. Her name was Judy Rankin. Though she never won a major, she won twenty-six LPGA tournaments and was a consistent top-ten player for much of her career, which ended in 1979. Her best years were 1976 and 1977, when she earned Player of the Year awards. In both of those years she finished second at the LPGA Championship—the closest she ever came to winning a major.

In three different seasons, she won the Vare Trophy for the lowest scoring average. In 1976, she became the first female professional golfer to earn more than $100,000 in a single season. That year, she won six tournaments and earned in excess of $150,000.

For her efforts, she was elected into the World Golf Hall of Fame in 2000. Rankin still remains a force in women's golf, serving as an announcer for both ABC and ESPN. She is "one of the most recognizable voices in all of golf."[21]

Donna Caponi

Donna Caponi won twenty-four LPGA tournaments, including four majors. She won the U.S. Open in 1969 and 1970 and the LPGA Championship in 1979 and 1981. She won her four majors in three different decades. Amazingly, her first LPGA tournament was the prestigious U.S. Open—a title she defended the next year.

In her last major win—the 1981 LPGA—she sank a 15-ft putt for a birdie at the 72nd and final hole to earn a one-stroke victory. Her best years may have been 1980 and 1981—years in which she won five and four tournaments, respectively.

She was elected by the LPGA Veterans Committee to the LPGA Hall of Fame in 2001. "It's the most tremendous thing I could ever imagine," said the 56-year-old Caponi on her induction. "It just caps off my career, but more than anything, what makes this so meaningful is that it's the players voting for you and knowing they consider you of quality for the Hall of Fame."[22]

CHAPTER 7

NANCY LOPEZ

Ladies' golf is in existence for 30 years and has been ignored. We needed the shot in the arm she gave us. It's a very exciting time for ladies' golf; I'm sorry I'm not younger.

—Sandra Palmer[1]

Nancy Lopez has a real dignity about her, the aura of a Spanish queen.

—Dave Anderson[2]

You see, although we've had marvelous women golfers in the past, like Mickey Wright, up to now professional women's golf hasn't been important enough for sports writers to call any era "The Age of Somebody or the Other," as has happened in men's golf. In this century golf has seen "The Age of Bobby Jones," and of Ben Hogan, and of Arnold Palmer, and of Jack Nicklaus. But when they talk about the great women, the most they're apt to write is to stick in an adjective, like the "incomparable" Babe Didrikson Zaharias, or the "fabulous" Mickey Wright, or the "legendary" Patty Berg or Kathy Whitworth.

Well I'd like to leave behind me a record that would kind of demand that golfers will think of it as "The Age of Nancy Lopez." It may be too much to hope for. It may be too much to expect. It may be beyond my reach. But it's not too much to shoot for!

—Nancy Lopez[3]

Many times throughout history a particular sport needs that special star. In the late 1970s, as heavyweight great Muhammad Ali faded further from his peak, boxing needed a star and received one from the Montreal Olympic Games in 1976 through a fast and charismatic young welterweight named

Ray Charles Leonard, better known as "Sugar" Ray Leonard. Men's pro
fessional basketball needed stars in the 1970s and received a pair of great
rivals in Earvin "Magic" Johnson and Larry Joe Bird. Before the advent of
Bird and Magic, Julius Erving—Dr. J.—literally saved the NBA from
oblivion.

Arguably women's golf needed such a face-lift as well, given that the
women's game still suffered from a lack of exposure and lack of respect.
They had some great players but needed that charismatic star to transcend
the sport. One writer described the tour as one that "was puttering around
with a group of fine but aging veterans and sexy newcomers who excelled
in toothpaste commercials."[4] Enter Nancy Lopez. Famous sportswriter
and author Grace Lichtenstein wrote: "Every sport seems to need at least
one [superstar] in the scramble for television and sponsor dollars. Nancy
Lopez is that star, and she could not have come at a better time."[5]

Just after World War II, a Mexican-American named Domingo Lopez
entered trade school. He had come a long way through sheer hard work.
He quit school after the third grade to work in the cotton farms to help his
family of nine to do better in a small West Texas town called Valentine.

He landed a job in a shop owned by a man who had once been a first-rate
golf player. His boss taught Domingo how to play the game and Domingo
could not get enough of the game. He became nearly a scratch golfer and
enjoyed playing with his wife Mariana. Domingo and Mariana would often
go to a local course and take along their young daughter Nancy. While playing at the local Cahoon Golf Club, the couple dropped a ball and told their
young daughter to follow along. It turned out that Nancy was a natural. She
kept placing the ball near the hole. Her father was stunned—with joy. He
told his wife that Nancy would not do dishes: "Our Nancy will not do
any dishes. Her hands are meant for golf."[6] She would beat her father—a
3-handicapper—by the age of twelve.

"Daddy just put the ball on the ground and told me to hit it into the hole
way down there," she said. "That's about as formal a lesson as I've ever
had."[7] This lack of professional training explains a most unorthodox golf
swing for any golfer—much less for a future Hall of Famer. Nancy moved
her hands up the club as she drew back and made a huge loop over her head.
It was anything but textbook technique, but something unusual happened in
this child prodigy—she kept improving. As an 11-year-old, she entered the
women's state tournament and lost by a single stroke to the defending
champion. The next year at the age of twelve, she won the title by defeating
Mary Bryan by a whopping score of 10 and 8. The state's best women golfers shook their head in absolute amazement at the child prodigy. "It is the
greatest moment of my life," Nancy said.[8]

The victory at twelve was no fluke, as Nancy won the title again at ages
thirteen and fourteen. She still did not receive any professional coaching.
Her family as Mexican-Americans did not feel as they would welcome at

the local country club.[9] Her father Domingo served as her sole instructor. "She's been improving at the rate of three strokes a year and until she stops getting better, I don't think we should try and change her natural style," her father said.[10] No one could argue with Domingo on August 22, 1971, when Nancy won her third straight title at the age of fourteen by winning over 36 holes by an incredible score of 13 and 12 over an overmatched Donna Sauve. Nancy wondered whether she should change her unorthodox swing and once asked Lee Trevino, the great PGA legend, what she should do. Trevino replied: "You can't argue with success. If you swing badly but still score well and win, don't change a thing."[11]

At fifteen, Nancy Lopez turned her eyes on national tournaments. She gained national headlines in August 1972 when she captured the United States Golf Association's junior girls' title in Jefferson City, Missouri, by defeating Catherine Morse 1-up. The match was nip and tuck, with Lopez winning the last 2 holes to earn the narrow victory. On the 17th hole, Lopez sank a 30-ft putt to mark a continuing pattern in her career—the ability to produce great shots in the clutch. Lopez added a second national juniors title in August 1974 at the age of seventeen. In the meantime, Lopez played on the golf team at Goddard High School—the boys' golf team that won the state championship.

In 1975, an 18-year-old Lopez entered the professional U.S. Open championship as an amateur. Two months later she would attend Tulsa University and play golf there. In college, she received some lessons but they seemed to throw her off her game. "I can't swing like the picture players," Lopez said. "I took some lessons when I was at Tulsa and all it did was throw me off. I had to go back to my natural way."[12] Lopez later explained a key to her success: "I've never learned what it is you do when you hook or slice. I just swing to get it where I want it to go."[13] Hall of Famer Carol Mann, who later became an excellent television golf analyst, once referred to Lopez's unorthodox swing as a "combination of offsetting mistakes."[14]

But the U.S. Open told the world that a star had been born. Lopez was tied with Sandra Post after two rounds and eventually tied for second. She also finished second in a national juniors title in Tulsa, Oklahoma, falling to Beverley Davis of Jacksonville, Florida, by a score of 4 and 3. Lopez would gain a measure of revenge the next year by defeating Davis in the NCAA women's golf championship.

Lopez suffered personal tragedy when her mother died in September 1977. Lopez turned pro that year, citing a desire to test her skills against the best in the world and earn a good living. She would fulfill her and her late mother's dreams. Lopez became even more popular when she turned professional. Her natural charisma endeared her to throngs of spectators. Reminiscent of the great Arnold Palmer's fan base "Arnie's Army," throngs of fans began to form what some called "Nancy's Navy." She did not mind speaking with people at all:

When I walk from tee to green, I can talk to people and it doesn't bother me. I feel I'm in control. I like to have a relationship with the people because I want them to like me as a person. And I feel like the gallery can help you win by pulling for you. You can feel the vibrations.[15]

THE MAGICAL ROOKIE YEAR OF 1978

The LPGA tour sure felt the vibrations when Lopez turned pro. They may have felt a seismic shift, as Lopez turned in arguably the greatest two years of professional golf ever seen. When Lopez turned pro, a clinic featuring current LPGA players examined future pro golfers, including a young Nancy. After Nancy took a few swings, Jan Stephenson recalls she said: "Well, she's short and she's across the line, and she's never going to make it." Stephenson relates: "They've never let me forget that."[16]

In January 1978, Lopez showed more signs of things to come when she defeated the game's top player at the time, Judy Rankin, 4 and 2 in a match-play format. Lopez burst into tears of joy after defeating Rankin, thinking of her late mother. Rankin said of Lopez: "I don't think of Nancy Lopez as a rookie at match play."[17]

Lopez had come close on the tour with second-place finishes in majors but did not win her first title until February 1978—and rest was history. Lopez birdied the 17th hole in the final round to defeat Jo Ann Washam by one stroke at the Bent Tree tournament in Sarasota, Florida. Lopez dedicated the win to her late mother, saying she dearly wished that her mom could see her win an LPGA event. After her victory, Lopez said: "I'm still stunned. I'm real emotional and I started getting emotional on the course, knowing how bad I wanted to win for my mother."[18]

THE STREAK

Lopez's next tournament was in March at the Sunstar Tournament in Rancho Park, California. Lopez was five shots behind leader Debbie Austin in the final round, but managed to nail a long birdie on the 18th hole to win the tournament by a single shot. "I had an 18-foot foot putt and when I stood over it, I remembered the one I made at Bent Tree," Lopez said referring to her putt in her last tournament. "It was almost an identical putt and thinking about the one before made me feel good. When I stroked it I knew it was in all the way."[19] Her entire family—consisting of her father, sister, brother-in-law, niece, nephew, uncle, and aunt—all celebrated the victory in person. Lopez dedicated her second win to her father. Lopez nearly made it three in a row, finishing second to Sally Little in sudden-death play-off at the Honda Civic golf tournament in Rancho Bernardo, California. Little fired a final-round 65 to force the play-off and capture the title. Lopez, who herself shot a final-round 68, showed her characteristic good sportsmanship after the match, saying: "Sally shot a 65 and that's the way to lose. The play-off was a great experience for me. I'm just happy to have done as well as I have. Two firsts and a second isn't all that bad."[20]

Lopez proved prescient about the play-off experience, as she won in May in sudden death against one of her idols—JoAnne "Big Momma" Carner—at the LPGA Classic in Jamesburg, New York. The two finished at 3-under par, but Lopez's superior putting earned her the victory on the first play-off hole. "Beating Carner really makes me feel like a champion," Nancy said.[21] The victory at Jamesburg was Lopez's second straight win, as she had prevailed in Baltimore at her previous tournament.

The streak continued to three straight in New Rochelle, New York, at the hands of Carner again. "Big Momma" entered the final round with a three-stroke advantage, but Lopez entered the final round with a red hot putter. She shattered the record at the Wykagyl Country Club with a 65 to win by three strokes. "I felt good from my first tee," Lopez said. "I told Roscoe [her caddy] that if the putter felt as good in my hands as my clubs, I was going to play very well."[22]

The amazing streak continued in June at the LPGA Championship in Mason, Ohio. Lopez was not fazed by the major championship and was eager to continue her incredible run. Lopez shot 13-under par for the tournament, including a final-round 70 to win the tournament by six shots over fellow future Hall of Famer Amy Alcott. Lopez's first major title and fourth straight victory earned her numerous records, including the fastest to reach $100,000 earnings in a single season and the highest number of wins by a rookie player. "I owe it to my putter," Lopez said. Despite her incredible success, she remained humble, earning the respect of at least some of her peers. Alcott said: "I've never met a person who accepts what she does with such humility and class."[23]

Lopez won her fifth straight victory—an LPGA record—by winning the Rochester Classic with a come-from-behind victory over Jane Blalock and Debbie Massey. Blalock had a three-stroke lead heading into the final round, but Lopez fired a final-round 69 to capture the title. She once again proved magical with the putter, sinking a 30-ft birdie on the 17th hole. "She's the best putter I've ever seen in my life," gushed Blalock.[24] Blalock, herself a great golfer, added that she did not know how Lopez maintained her poise with the huge galleries following her every move on the course: "It's just tremendous, the pressure she's handled. You don't have a clue what that's like. And neither do I."[25]

Lopez's fifth win in a row made her the first woman to win five in a row. Mickey Wright, Kathy Whitworth, and Shirley Englehorn all had won four in a row, but no one had won five.

Some even wondered if perhaps Lopez could best the all-time record for consecutive wins held by the great Byron Nelson on the PGA tour, who won eleven in a row in 1945. When asked about the possibility of breaking the record, Lopez smiled and said, "I'd love to." Possibly the most amazing part of the streak was Lopez's brilliant putting. The famous saying, "drive for show and putt for dough" proved accurate for Lopez, who was uncanny during the streak. As one of her chief rivals, Jane Blalock, said: "Twenty-footers are gimmes for her. She's the best putter I've seen in my life."[26]

Debbie Massey, one of Lopez's rivals from her amateur days and on the LPGA tour, said: "I've never played with anyone who sank so many putts. I don't believe anybody on the men's tour is putting as well or as consistently as she is now."[27]

Lopez's streak ended at five in June 1978 at the Lady Keystone Open held at the Hershey Country Club in Hershey, Pennsylvania—the town where the great Wilt Chamberlain once scored 100 points in a pro basketball game. Lopez could conjure up no Chamberlainesque performance and edge closer to the Byron Nelson record. She finished far from the lead in the sixty-nine-woman field. Future Hall of Famer Pat Bradley captured the title with a 10-under par total, including a final-round 67. "I truly believe that if Nancy had been rested it would have been a much different story, a much tougher contest. She's worn out."[28] Lopez admitted that her concentration was not as focused as it was during the height of her amazing run. The crowd stayed with her throughout the week, groaning with every missed putt. A Hershey Country Club official spoke for most of the fans at the event: "Nancy Lopez is the grandest thing that's ever hit the L.P.G.A. I hope she can sleep five days straight and come back and knock them dead."[29]

Lopez's year earned her continued admiration among her fellow competitors and LPGA officials. Ray Volpe, the then LPGA commissioner said: "She has the sex appeal of Palmer and the charisma of Trevino." Judy Rankin, the tour's leading money winner in 1977, remarked: "They've got the wrong 'Wonder Woman' on TV."[30] Kathy Whitworth, the LPGA's all-time tournament winner with eighty-eight, remarked during Lopez's streak: "She's like on a tidal wave and I'm excited for her."

The "tidal wave" even caused some to speculate whether Lopez would try her hand at the men's events. In a letter to the editor in the *New York Times*, a gentleman wrote that "any tournament that bars Nancy will just be diminished by her absence."[31]

Lopez's dominance once caused a sportswriter at post-tournament press conference to call the tournament winner Jane Blalock "Nancy." The outspoken Blalock was less than pleased and commented that it was an "insult" to all the great women golfers to say that Nancy Lopez is women's golf.[32] Lopez became so dominant that people even started calling other young golfers "the next Nancy Lopez," including another future Hall of Famer Beth Daniel, who had actually eliminated Nancy at the 1975 U.S. Women's Amateur tournament.[33]

Given her dominance, many experts picked Lopez as an odds-on favorite to win the 1978 U.S. Women's Open. However, the women's game had many great players and no player—not even Lopez—could keep up that incredible pace. Hollis Stacy captured her second straight Open championship with a one-shot victory over JoAnne Carter and a fast-charging Sally Little, who fired a final-round 65. Lopez finished in a three-way tie for fifth with Peggy Conley and Sandra Post six strokes behind Stacy. Lopez was in good position after two rounds but fired a disastrous 79 in the third round to end her realistic chances.

In August, Lopez returned to her winning ways by capturing the European Women's Open in Sunningdale, England, by three strokes over JoAnne Carter, Sally Little, and Mary Dwyer. Lopez was a hit with the British fans who called her "Laughing Eyes." Lopez's win pushed her to more than $153,000 earnings for the year—besting the previous record set by Judy Rankin in 1977. Lopez set her sights on breaking Mickey Wright's record of thirteen tournaments in a year. "I'm really excited now," she said. "I guess I'll think about that 13th when I hit 12."[34]

Lopez failed to reach the heights set by the great Mickey Wright, but she did have one of the best seasons in LPGA history—before or since, winning nine tournaments, Rookie of the Year, Player of the Year, and the Vare Trophy for her lowest average score on tour. One writer editorialized: "Move over, Jack Nicklaus and Tom Watson. Make room for Nancy Lopez."[35] Her rookie year dominance earned a landslide victory for the Associated Press' coveted Athlete of the Year award. She received 336 of 412 votes— 309 votes ahead of second-place finisher tennis legend Chris Evert. She became the first golfer to win the award since 1966.

ANOTHER GREAT YEAR IN 1979

Sometimes sports stars have one great rookie year and then fade into mediocrity or at least never again reach those lofty peaks. The recent example in the sporting world was Detroit Tigers' rookie pitcher Mark Fidrych, known simply as "the Bird" for his resemblance to Big Bird with his huge curly hair. In his rookie season, Fidrych dominated baseball with nineteen wins, leading the league in earned run average and complete games. At times, "Bird" was unhittable. Unfortunately he suffered an injury the next year and was never the same, as he never won more than six games in another season.

Other great sports figures suffer from what is commonly known as the sophomore jinx—performing much less well in their second season than their first. Nancy Lopez trashed the myth of the sophomore jinx by posting another incredible season. She won eight of the nineteen tournaments she entered—a wining percentage unfathomable even to most great golfers. She managed to repeat her pattern of playing well in the clutch. In March,

she sank a 10-ft birdie putt to edge Hollis Stacy by one stroke to win the
Sunstar Classic in Los Angeles. Rumors circulated that some players, including Stacy, were openly cheering for anyone to win other than Lopez. Stacy
vehemently denied those rumors, saying: "You just can't say anything bad
about Nancy."[36]

Perhaps the most interesting of Lopez's eight tournament wins that year
came later in May at the Colonial National Invitational in Fort Worth,
Texas, where Lopez prevailed in sudden death over the legendary Mickey
Wright. The 44-year-old Wright played only part-time on tour but managed
to conjure up some of her old magic on this week. At the end of regulation,
an amazing five golfers—Wright, Lopez, Hollis Stacy, Jo Ann Washam, and
Bonnie Bryant—finished tied for first. At the first play-off hole, Wright
dropped her tee shot a mere 18 in. from the hole to birdie the par 3. Stacy,
Washam, and Bryant failed to birdie, leaving only Lopez with a chance to
remain in contention. In typical Lopez fashion, she sank an 18-footer to
birdie the hole. At the next play-off hole, Nancy sank a 10-ft putt to win
the championship. Wright had nothing but praise for her young opponent:
"Nancy's the finest champion to come along in many years. The girl will
win tournaments as long as she plays the game."[37]

Her competitors recognized that Lopez helped them all because she
brought more attention and, therefore, more sponsors to the LPGA. "Nancy
didn't build this tour, but she's built a lot of it in two years," said Pat
Bradley. "We have all benefited through Nancy. It's all for the good."[38]

Her performances in 1978 and 1979 caused many to speculate that she
should be considered amongst the greats of all time. Former LPGA great
Betsy Rawls even remarked in 1979 that Nancy was a better player than
the legendary Babe Didrikson:

Nancy is a better player than the Babe was. Her swing is better. She doesn't hit as
many bad shots. Babe was a tough competitor, but she didn't control herself as well
as Nancy does. Any time that Babe lost her composure, her game would suffer. I've
never seen that happen to Nancy.[39]

In October that year Lopez captured her eighth title of the year by
winning an LPGA tournament in Dallas, Texas, by two shots over Sandra
Post. Lopez's latest triumph pushed her season's earnings to more than
$190,000—breaking her own LPGA record from her rookie season. Lopez
had met sportscaster Tim Melton during her rookie year, and they married
within 6 months, in January 1979.

Lopez never won as much as she did in 1978 and 1979, but she remained
one of the game's top golfers for many years. In 1980 she won three tournaments, including a final-hole victory over "Big Momma" Carner at the
Rail Charity Classic in Springfield, Illinois. Carner entered the final round
with a two-stroke advantage, but Lopez proved better with the putter.

She holed a 10-ft birdie putt on the 18th to capture her twentieth career title. At twenty-three, she became the youngest player in history to win that many tournaments.

In 1981, she added three more tournament titles—the Arizona Copper Classic, the Colgate-Dinah Shore, and the Sarah Coventry titles. At the Colgate-Dinah Shore in Rancho-Mirage, Lopez began the final round three strokes behind Carolyn Hill but carded a final-round 64 (her career best) to win by two strokes. On this day, Lopez made four straight birdies from holes 12 to 15 to pull away from the field.

In 1982, Lopez won two tournaments—the J&B Scotch Pro-Am and the Mazda Japan Classic. At the Scotch Pro-Am in Las Vegas, Nevada, Lopez won by five strokes over Sandra Haynie. In the final round, Lopez held a nine-stroke advantage at one point and coasted to victory with a score of 73. "It makes me feel better to be back on top," she said. "This was a great tournament to start off winning again."[40]

Lopez was not winning as much. It may have something to do with off-the-course issues, as her marriage to Melton ended in 1982, when she filed for divorce. "I think marriages can work on the tour," she said. "But, I think in my case anyway, I was being shared with Tim and with everybody....It's not really like a successful woman in business. A businesswoman who does well is not shared the way a woman athlete is."[41]

Lopez did say that she wanted to marry again, and she did, to Houston Astros' baseball star Ray Knight. Reports surfaced of a possible romance but Lopez said they were just friends. In October 1982, she married Knight and the two have remained happily married for more than 25 years, having three children. The two had their first child, Ashley Marie, in 1983.

Motherhood affected Nancy's game. In 2002, she wrote for the *Golf for Women Magazine:* "After I had Ashley, it was hard for me to feel as competitive, as tough. Once I became a mother, the professional athlete got pushed to the side."[42]

She still managed to win two more tournaments in 1983, including the J&B Scotch Pro-Am for the second consecutive year. Lopez sank a 7-ft putt on the final hole to defeat Laura Baugh Cole by one shot. She won two more tournaments in 1984—the Uniden LPGA Invitational and the Chevrolet World Championship of Women's Golf.

Lopez vowed to return to the top of the game and she did just that in 1985—her finest year on tour besides her magical first 2 years in 1978 and 1979. That year, Lopez entered twenty-five tournaments and finished in the top ten an amazing twenty-one times. Fifteen times she finished in the top three—including five wins. She accomplished perhaps her greatest golfing feat that year in June 1985 when she won the LPGA Championship—the second of her three major championships—by eight strokes. In the third round, Lopez had received a two-stroke penalty for slow play and finished the day deadlocked with Alice Miller. Lopez seethed at the penalty and responded with one of the greatest rounds of golf in major championship history. She fired a 65 and crushed her competitors.

"I still don't think I should have gotten that penalty, and I was still mad today," Lopez said after her victory. "But I was really motivated, so I was mad in a positive way."[43] Lopez even managed to make light of the slow-play charge during her final round. On the final green, she asked out loud: "Does anybody know what time it is?" Someone from the gallery responded: "Take all the time you need."[44]

Lopez continued her winning ways in 1985 with a convincing ten-stroke victory at the Henreden Classic in Springfield, Illinois. She fired a final-round 66 to increase the lead on an overmatched field. "I've been playing very well, very consistently," she said. "But this was a week when everything fell together. Every time I got a chance to swing at the ball, it was going at the hole."[45]

In 1986, Lopez gave birth to her second daughter Erinn Shea. Her lifestyle consisted of far more than preparing for golf tournaments. She traveled with a nanny, a baby seat, and a playpen.[46] It was the first year on tour that Lopez did not win a tournament event, but that statistic is deceiving, as she only entered four tournaments. Of those four, she finished in the top three in three of them. She rebounded to play a bigger schedule and she won at least one tournament every year from 1987 through 1993. In 1987, she won the Sarasota Classic, giving her her thirty-fifth career title and an automatic induction into the LPGA Hall of Fame, which at that time set the bar at thirty-five career victories. She defeated Kathy Baker by three strokes to capture the title. She became the eleventh woman to earn such a distinguished honor. "You think about this day and strive to get it," she said, "but you wonder if it'll ever come. This is special, to get into the Hall of Fame where there are so many great players."[47]

She still managed displays of brilliance on the greens—just more infrequently than the early years. In May 1988, she won the Chrysler-Plymouth Classic by eight strokes over second-place finisher Jan Stephenson. Her final-round performance included a bogey-free round of 66 and she hit every green in regulation.

In 1989 Lopez won the last of her three majors at a familiar site—the LPGA Championship at Kings Island, Ohio. Lopez was two shots back after 10 holes but fired a final-round 66 to defeat Japan's Ayako Okamoto by three shots. Lopez was awesome on the back 9, chipping in for birdie at the 11th hole and sinking a 20-ft birdie putt at the 12th to take charge. She followed that with birdies at the 14th, 17th, and 18th holes for the championship. It was Lopez's fortieth career victory.

"I can't compare the victories here," she said. "The first was in my rookie year and was so exciting. Then the year of the two-shot penalty was so satisfying because it was a victory of justice for me at that time. Then this one was just special."[48] The performance of Lopez caused Okamoto to call her "the best woman golfer under the skies."

Lopez added six more titles after 1989 for a career total of forty-eight. Even at the age of forty in 1997, she had nine top-ten finishes and a victory at the MBS LPGA Classic title with a sudden-death play-off win. She had one second-place finish in 1998.

In 2002, after 25 years on the tour, Lopez played her last full season. At the age of forty-five, she received a hearty ovation as she played the U.S. Women's Open. The crowd at the Prairie Dunes Country Club gave her a standing ovation, while Hall of Famer Juli Inkster gave her a tip of her cap while playing. They were fitting gestures for the most popular player in LPGA history. Clifton Brown of the *New York Times* wrote: "No L.P.G.A. player has ever been more popular than Lopez, who connected with fans because of her magnetic personality."[49]

HER IMPACT

Lopez had an indelible impact on the game. Her competitors feared her. "Nancy Lopez happened to be there at the right time, as Commissioner Volpe was improving the tour," says fellow LPGA pro Janet Coles, who began around the same time as Lopez. "She had perfect timing in that sense and she won a lot of tournaments. She also had a great, marketable personality, similar to Arnold Palmer. Nancy was very daunting to play against. She was a very tough competitor, a Tiger-like player when she got near the top of the leaderboard."[50]

Her former coach at the University of Tulsa Dale McNamara said it best: "It used to be we would have girls who simply enjoyed the game of golf, but it didn't really fit into their lives. Now, they want to be like Nancy Lopez, and we have to help them."[51] Meg Mallon, an LPGA star in the 1990s and beyond, said that it was watching Nancy Lopez winning five tournaments in a row in 1978 that inspired her as a 16-year-old to first think about playing golf as a professional.

She not only inspired a generation of future women golfers, she also saved the game. She was that rare superstar athlete who had a magnetic personality, a kind heart, and a love of her fans. "Her Latina heritage brought new fans to the game."[52] Nancy Lopez was the Arnold Palmer of women's golf—the ultimate good will ambassador for the game.

Lopez may not be done with her playing career. In March 2007, she announced that even at the age of fifty she would play five or six LPGA tour events in 2007. As of September 2007, she played six LPGA tour events. "I know I have to get in real good shape to try to compete with the young girls, but I think I still have the mental capacity to go out there and play good golf," said Lopez, who had shed 30 pounds.[53]

CHAPTER 8

OTHER GREAT PLAYERS

Nancy Lopez was obviously the most charismatic player of her time, perhaps of all time. She captured the public's imagination with her captivating story, ebullient smile, amazing poise, and special persona. But there have been many other great players that played during that era. Here are a few of them.

JOANNE CARNER

JoAnne "Big Momma" Carner had an unusual career path for a woman's professional golfer in the 1960s. Most professional golfers turn pro at a relatively young age. Carner was the exception, as she played amateur golf for years, compiling an amazing five U.S. Women's Amateur championships—one short of Glenna Collett Vare's all-time record. She won the national title in 1957, 1960, 1962, 1966, and 1968.

In October 1969, Carner announced that she would turn professional at the age of thirty. "There were no new horizons for me in the amateur field," she said. "Naturally the pro tour offers a tremendous challenge, and I finally realized it was a challenge that I could not pass up."[1]

In her first year as a professional, Carner made a major impact. She won the Wendell-West Women's Invitational golf tournament with a play-off victory over Marilyn Smith. The next year in 1971 she won the U.S. Women's Open by seven strokes over distant second-place finisher Kathy Whitworth. "The Open really means that I beat the pros," Carner said. "I wanted to as an amateur and couldn't and I turned pro and have perfected my game a little better and finally did it, which makes me feel good."[2]

Carner often saved her best in the clutch moments, as in the 1971 Bluegrass Invitation Tournament, when she sank an amazing 25-ft eagle putt on the final hole to defeat Sandra Haynie by three shots. She won ten LPGA tournaments in play-offs, including the Peter Jackson Classic, where she sank a 17-ft birdie putt on the first sudden-death play-off hole to defeat Carol Mann. She won the 1976 Los Angeles Open in a play-off, when she managed to hit a 50-ft chip shot to defeat Sandra Palmer.

In 1976, she won her second U.S. Open title by defeating Palmer in an 18-hole play-off by two strokes. She had to battle her way out of the rough on both the 17th and 18th holes of the play-off round. "If you can't get out of rough, you can't win the Open," Carner said afterward. "Right now I feel great. When you win one Open maybe it is luck. But when you've won your second Open, you know you've arrived as a pro."[3] Palmer was more succinct: "She's really awesome."[4]

She often proved the nemesis of poor Sandra Palmer, as she victimized her again in a play-off at the 1978 Triple Crown Match Play tournament. Carner won the prestigious sixteen-woman field, only as a replacement for Carol Mann, who withdrew. In 1979, she rallied from four strokes back to end up in a five-person play-off with Chako Higuchi, Jan Stephenson, Donna Caponi, and Nancy Lopez. She won on the second play-off hole.

She had a great rivalry with Nancy Lopez in the late 1970s and early 1980s. In the first years of the 1980s, Carner was the best in the game, winning Player of the Year honors in 1981 and 1982; the Vare Trophy in 1981, 1982, and 1983; and garnering more prize money than her competitors. "She plays to win and thrives on pressure," said her caddie Dennis White. "I know she intimidates some of the top players by being there."[5]

In August 1982, she played her way into the Hall of Fame by winning the LPGA World Championship of Women's Golf by five strokes over Amy Alcott. Carner finished her career with forty-four LPGA tournament victories. Her friendly rival Nancy Lopez summed Carner up well:

Now we're talking about one of the really great ones. As JoAnne Gunderson she had the best record any amateur ever achieved before turning professional, which she did back in 1970. Always a tough fighter, she was super match player, and most amateur events are match play events. As a pro, she's consistently been a top-10 player and continues to dominate match play events when they're held. I literally idolized her when I was an amateur and now, playing against her on even terms, I still kind of do.[6]

JAN STEPHENSON

In the early 1980s, Jan Stephenson was a world-famous personality for her exploits both on and off the golf course. On the golf course, she collected three major championships—the 1981 Peter Jackson Classic, the 1982 LPGA Championship, and the 1983 U.S. Women's Open. The beautiful

Australian also garnered Rookie of the Year honors in 1974 for her outstanding play.

She may have been best known, however, for her off-course activities, including posing in sexy photos, being interviewed for *Playboy,* and becoming an international sex symbol—similar to Anna Kournikova in tennis years later. The difference was that Anna Kournikova could never win a major tournament in singles play, while Jan Stephenson could. She truly was a fierce competitor on the golf course and one of the best in her prime.

SALLY LITTLE

The South Africa–born Sally Little won two major championships and fifteen total tournament victories during her LPGA career. She captured the 1980 LPGA Championship and the 1988 du Maurier Classic. She burst on the scene in 1971, garnering Rookie of the Year honors. She won a tournament every year from 1978 to 1983. While her career win totals may pale in comparison to other great players, Little was known for her low-scoring final rounds. She fired a then record 65 in the final round of the 1978 U.S. Women's Open to finish second by one stroke. She fired a final-round 68 to win the 1982 Mayflower Classic. "Sally has had a dry spell lately but she's had her moments when no one could touch her," Beth Daniel said.[7]

SANDRA HAYNIE

Sandra Haynie won more than forty LPGA tour events, including four majors—the 1965 and 1974 LPGA Championship, the 1974 U.S. Women's Open, and the 1982 du Maurier Classic. She was a dominant player on the tour from 1962 to 1975 even though she had to compete against the fearsome twosome of Mickey Wright and Kathy Whitworth. In 1962, she won her first LPGA title at nineteen and captured her last title at the age of forty at the Rochester International.

She actually retired from golf for several years after 1975 and decided to return in 1980. In the meantime she served as a key counselor for the up-and-coming tennis superstar Martina Navratilova.

JANE BLALOCK

Jane Blalock holds the distinction for most LPGA tournament titles without a major victory. But she was a major force on the tour where she consistently won tournaments. All in all, she finished first twenty-seven times on tour. She won Rookie of the Year honors in 1969. In four different seasons—1972, 1974, 1978, and 1979—she won four tournaments. She retired from full-time competition in 1986 and runs a successful golf academy.

Blalock was nothing if not consistent. She made 299 consecutive cuts from 1969 to 1980. Janet Coles, a fellow LPGA professional who competed against Blalock, said she was one of the best players she ever played against. "She was a great competitor," Coles said.[8]

HOLLIS STACY

Hollis Stacy won eighteen LPGA tournaments and four majors—the 1977 U.S. Open, the 1978 U.S. Open, the 1983 du Maurier, and the 1984 U.S. Open. She won at least one tournament every year from 1977 through 1985.

It should have been no surprise that she was a success on the LPGA tour, given her incredible amateur record dating back to her junior days. She won three straight United States Golf Association Junior Championships in 1969, 1970, and 1971 from ages fifteen to seventeen. She first became only the second player (the first was Judy Eller in 1957 and 1958) to repeat as champion[9] and then became the first player to ever win three straight national titles. In her third championship, she defeated Amy Alcott by sinking a 10-ft birdie putt on the 19th hole.[10]

PAT BRADLEY

For single great seasons of golf, Pat Bradley's campaign in 1986 must be ranked near the top of the list. That year she won five tournaments, including three of the four majors: the Kraft Nabisco, the LPGA Championship, and the du Maurier Classic. She won three other majors: the 1981 U.S. Women's Open, the 1981 du Maurier Classic, and the 1985 du Maurier Classic.

She suffered from hyperthyroidism, or Grave's Disease, in 1987 and 1988, which virtually knocked her out completely from competitive golf. She recovered to win one tournament in 1989, three tournaments in 1990, and four tournaments in 1991.

"I may not be up there attracting publicity or may not be a household name," Bradley has said. "I may be far behind in superstar quality, not as acceptable as some others, but in facts and figures, I'm up there with the greats."[11]

JULI INKSTER

In 1983 a young rookie in only her fifth LPGA tournament defeated the great Kathy Whitworth to win the Safeco Classic. This youngster trailed the great Whitworth by five strokes headed into the final round. Her name was Juli Inkster. Like Kathy Whitworth, she would eventually make it to the Hall of Fame for her golfing exploits.

It should have come as no surprise to golfing experts that Inkster had a solid professional career given that she dominated amateur golf, winning three straight U.S. Women's Amateur titles from 1980 to 1982. She represented the United States in the Curtis Cup and earned all-American honors at San Jose State.

She has won seven majors in her illustrious career—the 1984 and 1989 Dinah Shore Classics, the du Maurier Classic in 1994, the U.S. Women's Open in 1999 and 2002, and the LPGA Championship in 1999 and 2000.

Perhaps her most improbable triumph came at the age of forty-two at the 2002 U.S. Women's Open where she outshot the great Annika Sorenstam to capture her seventh major title. "She won with a Houdini-like wedge and a hot putter," wrote one reporter.[12]

In 2006, at the age of forty-five, she still remains a threat on the LPGA tour. She won the Safeway International that year and also carded a low-round of 63 that year. She will continue to add to her Hall of Fame resume.

AYAKO OKAMOTO

Ayako Okamoto won sixty-two tournaments worldwide. She was by far and away the best Japanese golf player, dominating the LPGA of Japan with more than forty tournament victories. But she wanted to test her skills against the very best so she traveled to the LPGA and faced off against the best in the United States and the rest of the world. She did not disappoint, winning seventeen LPGA tour events. "She had wonderful hand-eye coordination and an imaginative short game," said Hall of Famer Juli Inkster. "I would pick her over anybody and she was one of the best putters out here."[13]

She never won an LPGA major championship but she came very close. She lost in an 18-hole play-off to Laura Davies for the 1987 U.S. Women's Open championship. Perhaps the most remarkable fact is that she started playing golf at the relatively ancient age of twenty-two.[14]

AMY ALCOTT

Amy Alcott has won twenty-nine LPGA tournaments, including five majors. She captured the 1979 du Maurier Classic, the 1980 U.S. Women's Open, the 1983 Kraft Nabisco Championship, the 1988 Kraft Nabisco Championship, and the 1991 Kraft Nabisco Championship. She captured the 1975 Rookie of the Year award and won the 1980 Vare Trophy for the lowest scoring average.

For years she was just short of qualifying for the Hall of Fame, because the LPGA tour required thirty career wins for admission. Alcott was stuck on twenty-nine wins for many years. In 1992 she stated:

Basically, I feel like I'm in my own Hall of Fame. It's important. Maybe to other players it's the pinnacle. But if something happened to me tomorrow and I couldn't play golf again, I'd feel very satisfied with what I've done. I've won tournaments all over the world, and I've won them in just about every way. I don't need someone assigning me a number to let me know I've had a successful career.[15]

In February 1999 the LPGA changed its Hall of Fame criteria from requiring thirty tournament titles with two majors to a new system that requires a player to earn twenty-seven points.[16]

BETSY KING

Betsy King won six major championships and a total of thirty-four LPGA tournaments in her Hall of Fame career. She captured the Nabisco Dinah Shore in 1987, 1990, and 1997; the U.S. Women's Open in 1989 and 1990; and the LPGA Championship in 1992. She overcame a three-shot deficit in the Nabisco Dinah Shore to win her last major in 1997. In 1993, she won the Vare Trophy, the Rolex Player of the Year award, and topped the LPGA's money list.

King was a great athlete, playing basketball in high school and at Furman University for 2 years until she switched to golf. Her love of basketball continued during her professional golf days. She served as a volunteer assistant coach for a high school basketball team during the LPGA off-season. She helped lead Furman to the 1976 NCAA championship in golf.

BETH DANIEL

In 2003, a 46-year-old woman set a record by becoming the oldest woman to ever win on the LPGA tour. Her name was Beth Daniel—she burst on the professional scene in 1979 as the "next Nancy Lopez," garnering Rookie of the Year honors. The next year in 1980 she won four tournaments and captured Player of the Year honors. She suffered a slump between 1985 and 1989. She failed to win a tournament for three straight years from 1986 to 1988.

In 1983, she won the LPGA Kids' Classic with a sudden-death play-off win over JoAnne Carner. "In playoff golf it's do or die," she said. "You have to give it your best shot. If it works, it works. If it doesn't, it doesn't."[17] Of her thirty-three tour victories, she won only one major championship—the 1990 LPGA Championship. But it was an amazing performance. She fired a final-round 66 to edge Rosie Jones by one stroke. Television announcer and former men's PGA great Johnny Miller said: "If Arnold Palmer was shooting this score they'd be doing cartwheels in the gallery. This is one great round of golf."[18] Jan Stephenson said in a recent interview that the best player of her generation was Beth Daniel because she "stood the test of time."[19]

PATTY SHEEHAN

Patty Sheehan has won thirty-five LPGA tour events, including six major championships: the 1983, 1984, and 1993 LPGA Championship, the 1992 and 1994 U.S. Women's Open, and the 1996 Nabisco Dinah Shore Classic. She began her athletic career as a downhill skier, the best in the country as a young teenager. She turned to golf in college at the University of Nevada–Reno. She earned Rookie of the Year honors in 1981 and Player of the Year honors in 1983. Arguably, her best year was in 1990 when she won five tournaments.

LAURA DAVIES

The long-hitting Laura Davies has won twenty LPGA tournaments, including four major championships. These include the 1987 Women's Open, the 1994 LPGA Championship, the 1996 LPGA Championship, and the 1996 du Maurier Championship. She earned Player of the Year honors in 1996 after winning two majors in the same year. She plays with a go-for-broke attitude, blasting monstrous drives off the tee, far outdistancing her competitors. When her short game matches her prodigious driving ability, she can still compete with the best in the world.

MEG MALLON

Meg Mallon has won eighteen LPGA tournaments, including four majors. Those majors include the 1991 LPGA Championship, the 1991 U.S. Women's Open, the 2000 du Maurier Classic, and the 2004 U.S. Women's Open. Her last major she won at the age of forty-one. She is one of only six women to win the LPGA Championship and the U.S. Women's Open in the same year.

CHAPTER 9

THE LPGA SAILS UPWARD, GOES GLOBAL, AND WITNESSES A GREAT RIVALRY

In the 1980s the LPGA struggled a bit, as the Men's Senior Tour took off and siphoned away corporate dollars. Unlike the women, the male players over fifty now had another place to continue their lucrative playing careers. It is still a disparity that exists, as the women do not have a comparable seniors' tour.

But throughout the 1980s, there was a concern that the LPGA was not doing all it could with its sponsors and marketing. Ray Volpe had been a very effective commissioner in the 1970s before he left for a job in sports marketing. Former LPGA player Janet Coles said:

Ray Volpe was the commissioner that took the LPGA tour to another plane. He took us off the rural map and did an incredible job for women's golf. He took the women's tour from $2 million a year in prize money to more than $9 million. Because of his efforts some women players became millionaires.[1]

He was replaced by John Laupheimer, who did a good job in many respects but did not meet all expectations with respect to marketing, as the LPGA schedule had to reduce its number of tournaments. William Blue replaced Laupheimer in 1988, but his reign did not last long. Blue allegedly did not mesh well with tournament sponsors. The *New York Times* reported: "Blue, who was hired for his expertise in marketing, mixed a slick public presentation with a brusque interpersonal manner that ended up alienating him from sponsors and players and left him open to charges of questionable integrity."[2]

After Blue resigned under pressure, the LPGA needed a serious face change. One news account from 1990 read: "The Ladies Professional Golf Association wants more from its next commissioner—more tournaments, more TV coverage, more sponsors, more prize money and more vision."[3]

LPGA President Judy Dickinson wisely selected Charlie Mechem, a Yale-educated lawyer who was chairman and chief executive of Taft Broadcasting for years and a cosponsor of a leading LPGA tournament for years. It turned out to be the perfect choice. Author Jim Burnett writes in his book *Tee Times: On the Road with the Ladies Professional Golf Tour:* "By the time Mechem's five-year term was up, he had poured a foundation of solid steel for the LPGA."[4]

Mechem stepped into the job and said from the beginning that he would serve for 5 years. "When I first accepted the commissioner job, I said that I would only do the job for five years and that is what I did," he said in a personal interview. "I said I would step down on December 31, 1995."[5]

Mechem saw serious problems when he took over the helm.

What I sensed when I became commissioner was that the major problem facing the LPGA tour was a massive institutional inferiority complex born of several factors: (1) difficult times with sponsor defections; (2) an inferiority complex that afflicts women athletes because of the way the public perceives them; and (3) the [men's] senior tour was just really coming to its apex.[6]

Mechem told the LPGA players to focus on being the best they could be and not to worry about the PGA or the Senior PGA. "I told the ladies when I first spoke to them: 'We can't affect what the PGA Tour or the Senior Tour does or doesn't do. But we can impact what we do and will carry our heads high, look good, play the best golf we can and come out fighting every week.'"

Mechem made an important strategic decision that he says years later was "even better idea than I thought it would be." That idea was to attend every single LPGA tournament.

It exposed me to the four important constituencies: (1) fans, (2) players, (3) the media; and (4) the sponsors. I realized that I needed to be visible with the sponsors in part because the women's golf game doesn't pop obviously into people's minds. I felt I needed to help build loyalty among the sponsors.

Mechem and Dickinson (whom he readily credits) accomplished much during his term as commissioner.

I am most proud of the following four things: (1) overcoming the inferiority complex and making the LPGA a respected force in sports and the players proud of their organization; (2) creating the LPGA Foundation so that we would have a charitable foundation; (3) starting the rookie program, which obligated all rookies to spend two days as a volunteer at any tournament; and (4) create the first traveling child care program in the history of professional sports.[7]

The job was difficult, as Mechem soon discovered, because of pervasive gender bias. He was surprised at this discrimination.

I grew up in a small town in Southern Ohio called Nelsonville. I'm a white Protestant male who went to a state university and I really never felt any discrimination. I wasn't in any of the categories of people that normally faced such discrimination. But, I began to feel discrimination by osmosis with respect to sponsors pulling out of obligations at the last minute citing unspecified budgetary concerns. I realized something was happening here that wasn't quite right. I think it was a prejudice against women's golf born out of an attitude that women were inferior athletes or the lesbian issue.[8]

The lesbian issue hit center stage after a story written by Valerie Helmbreck for the *Wilmington News Journal* quoting famed CBS golf broadcaster Ben Wright. Wright allegedly said things such as: "Let's face facts here. Lesbians in the sport hurt women's golf. They're going to a butch game and that furthers the bad image of the game. Women are handicapped by their boobs....Their boobs get in the way." Wright denied making the remarks and CBS defended him. "I am disgusted at the pack of lies and distortion that was attributed to me," Wright said. A subsequent investigation by *Sports Illustrated* indicated that Helmbreck was telling the truth, not Wright. CBS then fired Wright. In May 1998, Wright apologized to Helmbreck and admitted he made what he called "stupid" remarks.[9]

Mechem was commissioner when the imbroglio occurred and he was "sickened" by the comments.

I was outraged at the lesbian issue because it made me sick to think that people would talk about players' sexual orientation and say, "Is she or isn't she?" It just shouldn't be an issue. They are world-class golfers and they should be measured by that standard. I really laid down the law after the Ben Wright controversy. I thought it was idiotic that everyone was talking about those comments instead of the great golf being played.[10]

Mechem did not realize that so many people would focus on the lesbian issue. "I always acknowledged there was a mix of lifestyles in women's sports but didn't fully realize that some people had a problem with that."[11]

Despite the Wright controversy, Mechem's tenure marked a period of growth and prosperity on the women's tour. Another positive development during his reign was that the tour became more global, as many great players came from many different countries. "That was simply an evolutionary thing," he says. "Many countries—such as Sweden and South Korea—began developing sophisticated programs from young women. Also, many players from other countries wanted to come to the LPGA tour not only for the money but also for the opportunity to challenge themselves against the best players in the world."[12]

"These things feed on themselves," he added. "[Swedish golfer] Lisalotte Neuman's success was a big inspiration for Annika Sorenstam and other Swedish women. I think the success of Se Ri Pak really inspired many young would-be women golfers in South Korea. The same thing will likely happen in Mexico with the success of Lorena Ochoa."[13]

A GLOBAL GAME

The LPGA has become a global game. Most of the dominant players in the game are not from the United States or Great Britain. The great Annika Sorenstam hails from Great Britain, the super Karrie Webb comes from Australia, and then there is the influx of great players from Asia. Numerous great players have come from South Korea, starting with a young player named Se Ri Pak, who had perhaps the most memorable rookie year on the LPGA tour since Nancy Lopez 20 years earlier. Those three women—Sorenstam, Webb, and Se Ri Pak—have been the three dominant female golfers for the past decade. All three already have qualified for the LPGA Hall of Fame even though they still either at or near the peaks of their games.

Not everyone, however, has been pleased with certain aspects of the global game. Former LPGA major winner Jan Stephenson said in a November 2003 interview with *Golf Magazine* when asked if there were other problems with the LPGA tour:

This is probably going to get me in trouble, but the Asians are killing our tour. Absolutely killing it. Their lack of emotion, their refusal to speak English when they can speak English. They rarely speak. We have two-day pro-ams where people are paying a lot of money to play with us, and they say hello and goodbye. Our tour is predominantly international and the majority of them are Asian. They've taken it over.[14]

However, others believe that the international aspect of the game is exciting and a positive development. Pam Swensen, chief executive officer of the Executive Women's Business Association, says:

It is truly an international sport with a uniformity of rules, etiquette and traditions that one can respect. I find the "internationalization" of the sport very exciting as we look to expand our organization into other parts of the world. Golf is a unifying sport; a quality sport; a sport of integrity and ethics. To me, those are universal qualities that everyone can honor. It is a bridge building opportunity. Competitions like the Solheim Cup, Ryder Cup, President's Cup generate international awareness for this great game which does impact interest at the grassroots level from both a fan perspective and a playing perspective. If you attend a U.S. Women's Open event, it is so exciting to see so many fantastic female golfers from around the world competing. And in the gallery, you will see excited younger boys and girls among their parents eagerly engaged in the action. They are the future of the game.[15]

A GREAT RIVALRY AND A TRULY DOMINANT PLAYER

In the 1990s and into the first decade of the twenty-first century, two women from different continents other than North America have dominated the LPGA in a way reminiscent of the Babe and Berg 40–50 years earlier. These two remarkable athletes are Sweden's Annika Sorenstam and Australia's Karrie Webb. Between them they have won 17 major tournaments and 104 LPGA victories. They have taken golf to levels never before seen. Sorenstam has fired an LPGA-record 59, while Webb has carded a nearly as impressive 61. At times the two dominated women's professional golf and made major tournaments their own personal rivalry. The *New York Times* reported that they had "ushered in a new era" of women's golf.[16] They have traded the world number one ranking every year from 1995 to 2005. Sorenstam finished number one in 1995, 1997, 1998, and 2001–2005. Webb has finished the year number one in 1996, 1999, and 2000. Sorenstam had established herself as the game's number one player in 1995, but then Webb burst onto the scene—first with an amazing win in the 1995 British Open and then capturing Rookie of the Year and Player of the Year honors in 1996.

ANNIKA SORENSTAM

Admit it. Almost everyone who likes golf, and many who don't, would be interested in watching Sorenstam play against the men, even those who don't believe she should have been given an exemption.

—Clifton Brown[17]

Called the "female Tiger Woods," Sorenstam has performed at such a high level for so long that many people now say that she is the greatest female professional golfer of all time. She has won sixty-nine tournaments, only nineteen tournaments shy of tying Kathy Whitworth for the all-time lead. She claims that it would be "impossible" of passing Whitworth's career mark but the numbers say otherwise.

Born in Sweden, Sorenstam became a tennis phenom as a youngster. Her parents pushed her to practice all the time. This burned out young Annika from tennis and she turned her energies on golf. It was a good career move. She played collegiately at the University of Arizona, winning the 1991 individual NCAA championship title. She played one LPGA event in 1992 and three events in 1993, but her first full rookie year was in 1994, when she played eighteen events. She earned the Rolex Rookie of the Year award for her performances that year, as she made the cut in fourteen of eighteen events.

In 1995, Sorenstam finished the year as the number one player in the world, winning the U.S. Women's Open and two other tournaments. She had three second-place finishes as well. She finished the U.S. Open with a final-round 68 to defeat Meg Mallon for her first career major win. However, the next year star rookie Karrie Webb stole her thunder by winning four times, finishing second five times and finishing the year as number one. That just motivated Sorenstam to return to even better form in 1997 and regain her status as the best player in the world. "I saw what Karrie did in 1996 and said, 'OK, it's time for me to go home, practice, and get better,'" she said. "It's not a mean rivalry, but we both bring out the best in each other."[18]

In 1997, Sorenstam won six tour events and finished second five other times. She topped $1.2 million in earnings and regained her number one world ranking. She also finished in the top ten an amazing sixteen times.

In 1998, she again repeated as the number one player in the world, winning four events with four second-place finishes. In July, she won the JAL Big Apple Classic with a performance for the ages. She fired four straight rounds in the 60s—67, 66, 65, and 67—for a tournament-record 265. She won the tournament by eight strokes. One newspaper reporter wrote: "It was a remarkable performance and a testament to the consistency that Sorenstam—acknowledged as the premier women's golfer—is able to maintain."[19]

In 1999 and 2000, Sorenstam had a "slump" by her standards—namely, she lost her world number one ranking. She finished at number four in 1999 and number two in 2000, as her rival Karrie Webb ascended to the top of the game. What was worse to Sorenstam was that she missed the cut at the 1999 U.S. Women's Open.

In March 2001, in Phoenix, Arizona, she had the most impressive single day scoring-wise of any golfer in history, as she fired a 59 at the Moon Valley Country Club in tournament play. She birdied 12 of her first 13 holes. She reminisced on the famous round in 2005 with *Golf Magazine*:

I remember the start because it was so incredible. I birdied the first eight holes. The shots weren't really that great, but it was the flow to it all and the momentum just kept building and building. I could do nothing wrong that day. Everything funneled to the green. Every putt had the right pace.[20]

She later added a major by winning the Kraft Nabisco Championship. Her torrid play earned her four straight victories. She failed to tie Nancy Lopez's record of five straight after falling to Se Ri Pak at the Longs Drug Challenge. However, her peers recognized her unique talents. Juli Inkster said: "She's playing awesome golf. Knowing Annika, she'll start another streak."[21] She won eight events in 2001 and had six second-place finishes. She finished in the top ten in twenty of the twenty-six events she played. She set a career record for low scoring average at 69.42 and earned more than $2 million —an LPGA record. She closed the year with a 65 at the Tyco/ADT Championship to finish two strokes behind Webb. But that did not detract from her great final round and a fabulous year. "I'm walking on clouds," she said. "Knowing the conditions and the course, I knew it would be tough. But, I wasn't going to let go if I had a chance."[22]

Amazingly, Sorenstam had an even better year in 2002, winning eleven tournaments and garner more than $2.8 million in prize money. She started the year winning six of the first twelve tournaments. Clifton Brown wrote: "Sorenstam has done what seemed almost inconceivable: she has taken her domination of the L.P.G.A. Tour to an even higher level, leaving opponents shaking their heads and observers in awe."[23]

In 2003, Annika Sorenstam played the Colonial tournament in Fort Worth, Texas. She became the first woman to play in a PGA tour event since the Babe in 1945. "I'm not here to prove anything," Sorenstam said. "I'm here to test myself."[24] She has stated that she wishes the men and women could play more often: "I wish we could do more with the guys because we all play the same game. Why not mix once in a while?"[25]

She did not make the cut, but earned the respect of the sports world and many male professionals. She claims it was the greatest moment of her career, competing against the men. "I decided to play in January of that year, so it was about four months of preparation: the physical training, working on the short game, preparing to deal with all the tension and expectations of playing in a men's event."[26] Her participation did not please all male golfers. Vijay Singh, one of the top men's players in the world, reacted quite negatively, saying: "I hope she misses the cut. Why? Because she doesn't belong out here. If I'm drawn with her, which I won't be, I won't play. What is she going to prove by playing? It's ridiculous."[27] Golf analyst David Feherty made a good point, though, when he noted that many more people would go to the Colonial to watch Annika rather than Vijay.[28]

Sorenstam played admiringly, carding a 71 and 74 for a 4-over par and missed the cut. She remained positive, stating: "I've climbed as high as I can and it's worth every step of it."[29] "What's wonderful is that we have this speculation in advance and get to see it play out," said Mary Jo Kane, a sociology professor at the University of Minnesota. "The question is no longer, 'Can women play?' The critical question is, 'At what level.' That's the 21st century question."[30]

The temporary move to the PGA did not harm Sorenstam's game when she returned to the LPGA, as she won the Kellogg-Keebler Classic in

Aurora, Illinois, in her first tour event after the Colonial media spectacle. She fired a 62, 66, and 71 to win by two strokes over Mhari McKay.

Sorenstam continued her stranglehold over the tour's top spot in 2004 and 2005, garnering more than $2.5 million in prize money each year. She won eight events in 2004 and ten events in 2005. At the beginning of 2004, she announced that she wanted the grand slam: "Everything is focused on the majors. Winning all four in one season is something that has never been done before, but I definitely think it is possible."[31] She won the LPGA Championship and finished second at the Open.

In 2005, Sorenstam began the year as if she would accomplish her greatest goal—to win the grand slam, or all four majors in the same calendar year. She won the Kraft Nabisco and the LPGA Championship to go 2 for 2, but finished in a disappointing twenty-third in the U.S. Women's Open.

Juli Inkster said in 2005: "I think Annika is the best player in the world. As far as consistency week in and week out, she's probably one of the most dominant athletes right now. I think everybody on the tour knows it. It'd be great if everybody else knew it."[32] Charlie Mechem, former LPGA commissioner, says:

Clearly she was the most dominant player in all of golf for a period of time. As one player told me: "Heck Charlie, she wins every other week." She didn't win quite that much but she was truly dominant. She is also a very classy, sophisticated woman who by her presence has been really good for the game.[33]

She captured her tenth major title at the U.S. Women's Open by defeating Pat Hurst by four strokes in an 18-hole play-off. It was her first Open victory in 10 years; "10 long years," according to Sorenstam. "It's been 10 years—10 long years. But I'm very, very grateful."[34] She fell to number three in the world rankings. Injuries have slowed her a bit, but every LPGA golfer feels the pressure every time that Sorenstam creeps up the leaderboard.

KARRIE WEBB

A 4-year-old Karrie Webb was handed plastic golf clubs by her grandparents, who waited until she was eight before they gave her a real set. It turned out to be quite a gift, as this precocious Australian continues to write her name in the record books with amazing performances.

She played one LPGA event in 1995, and it was one for the ages. The 20-year-old won the British Open by six strokes, a performance that set the stage for her record-breaking rookie year of 1996 when she earned more than $1 million in prize money and finished in the top ten an amazing ten times with five wins. She qualified for the LPGA tour by finishing second in the LPGA qualifying tournament with a broken wrist.

Since that time, Webb has remained a fixture in the game's elite, with her best run between 1999 and 2001, when at one stretch she won five out of eight major titles—a statistic that stacks up with any of the game's great players. "For those two years when she was in the field, everyone felt like they were playing for second place," said Juli Inkster.[35] She qualified for the World Golf Hall of Fame at twenty-five—the youngest in the history of the game.

CHAPTER 10

THE PAK ATTACK AND THE FUTURE OF WOMEN'S GOLF

For several years in the mid-1990s, what everyone talked about was that the LPGA was a two-woman duel between Sweden's Annika Sorenstam and Australia's Karrie Webb. These two were clearly far superior to the rest of the field. From 1995 to 1997, they were ranked the number one and two players in the world. Their domination seemingly would be inevitable. But, in 1998, another golfer burst onto the LPGA scene, putting together a phenomenal rookie season—a rookie season for the ages. Her name was Se Ri Pak. In 1998, she unleashed what some would call "the Pak Attack."

SE RI PAK

There is plenty of talk about Tiger Woods' impact on golf, and rightfully so. There is lots of talk about Michelle Wie's impact on golf, and rightfully so. But it's hard to find an athlete who has had more influence on the sport than Se Ri Pak. The PGA Tour still does not have a great deal more African Americans or Asians than it did when Tiger arrived on the scene....But Pak has single-handedly changed golf.

—Eric Andelman[1]

Right now, she's a national heroine. People call her the Joan of Arc right now for Korea, because she has done so much for people's morale, and for their confidence.

—Sung-Yong Steven Kil[2]

In 1978, Nancy Lopez, a young woman of Latino heritage, took the golf world by storm with her historic season. Twenty years later another young woman from a different part of the globe made a similar splash in her rookie season. This young woman's favorite sports athlete and idol was Nancy Lopez. In May 1998, this poised 20-year-old LPGA rookie took the tour by storm by completing a wire-to-wire victory in the McDonald's LPGA championship. This rookie fired a final-round 68 to complete her rounds in an impressive 11-under par—three strokes ahead of her nearest competitors. The victor was South Korea's Se Ri Pak.

The victory inspired a nation and led to a wave of fellow South Koreans coming to the LPGA tour. The story began years ago when Joon Chul Pak, a fine golfer in his own right, saw something special in his second daughter Se Ri. One day when Joon was playing golf, his fourth-grade daughter Se Ri asked to try the game. After 30 minutes, the young girl swung a golf club in nearly perfect fashion. Joon was ecstatic. He had a difficult time in his life, having been stabbed seventeen times by two men who were his former partners. Joon said he used to be "thug."[3] Reports surfaced that he had ties to organized crime, while Joon referred to his past as "hooliganism." Whatever his past, Joon saw a bright future for his second daughter.

Unfortunately for the driven Joon, his daughter seemed more interested in other sports, as she excelled in various track and field activities. He took his daughter to a local junior tournament when she was fourteen. The strategy worked, as daughter and father set their sights on a new goal—become the best female golfer in the world.

Beginning at the age of fourteen, Pak began to train incessantly—at least 6 hours a day. She woke up at 5:30 a.m. and ran up and down steps for conditioning and discipline. Joon's training methods have become the stuff of infamous lore. He hit her with a stick called a *pechori* when she made a bad shot.[4] He allegedly took her to a cemetery to develop mental toughness. He even made her spend the night in the cemetery. "Sometimes it got scary," she said. "Especially when it got really dark, and I had to walk home alone."[5]

Neighbors thought Joon was crazy for pushing his daughter so hard. Se Ri's mother worried that her husband was pushing her daughter too hard. But Joon had a dream that his daughter would be a world champion. Joon said: "I was very straight, very stern with Se Ri about her golf because I believed she had the talent, the patience to one day be a great player in the world."[6] Others assessed Joon differently, thinking his training methods excessive. One American newspaper wrote: "Compared to Joon Chul Pak, some might say Tiger Woods' father [the late Earl Woods] more closely resembles the benevolent, unobtrusive TV dad, Ward Cleaver."[7]

Joon defended his training methods as a necessary means to instill the mind-set of a champion—as someone who would not be intimidated under pressure. "I had to teach her how tough life is, that you must be the best in order to survive," Joon said. "That you must be steel-hearted and strong psychologically."[8]

Joon sacrificed financially, scraping together a large amount of money to buy a membership at a local country club in Seoul. Se Ri improved at a rapid rate. The family faced some discrimination due to social status, as some country club elites looked down on Joon perhaps because of rumors of his connections to the underworld.

At one tournament, he tried to introduce himself to the parents of other players. The other parents snubbed him. "They completely ignored me," Joon said.

I guess my daughter and myself didn't seem like much to them, because of their high social status. So I called Se Ri in front of her trophy and handed it to her, saying, "This is yours." The others looked at me as if I was some crazed lunatic. So I screamed back: "So what if I touch it! My Se Ri is going to take it home with her anyways?"[9]

Se Ri won more than thirty amateur tournaments over the next 4 years. She garnered attention at the October 1994 world team amateur title. In the last round, Pak shot a course-record 65, though the team from the United States won the championship. The English newspaper the *Times* referred to Se Ri's final-round show as the "Pak attack."[10]

In 1995, Se Ri traveled with her father to the United States for the U.S. Amateur Championship. She played very well, advancing to the semifinals before losing to Kelli Kuehne. She turned professional in Korea in 1996 and finished first or second in all fourteen tournaments she entered. She became a sports hero in her native country. But she yearned to prove herself on the world's biggest stage in golf—the LPGA.

She played a few LPGA events in 1997, making the cut in five of seven events. But it was 1998—her official rookie season—that Se Ri became an overnight international sensation. She began slowly that year with her best finish a mere eleventh place finish at the Longs Drug Challenge. Then, came the 1998 LPGA Championship. The 20-year-old Se Ri opened the tournament with a mind-boggling 65 followed by a second-round 68 and a third-round 68 to finish 11-under par—three strokes better than Donna Andrews and Lisa Hackney. It was a wire-to-wire victory. The others could not catch her and they realized it.

"She had her game face on, and she didn't let the pressure get to her," Andrews said. "I think a lot of the overseas players, especially the Japanese and the Koreans, are used to having so much media attention that they are not bothered when they are at the top of the leaderboard."[11]

Se Ri Pak added a second major in 1998 at the U.S. Women's Open in a classic at the brutal course at Blackwolf in Kohler, Wisconsin. Pak carded a 69 in round one, followed by a 70 in round two, which put her atop the leaderboard. The third round Se Ri carded a 76 in a gust-filled day. She maintained a one-shot lead. The fourth and final round featured similarly tough conditions. It was a brutal day of survival on the golf course. Se Ri managed to hold onto a slim lead until a virtual unknown, amateur Jenny Chuasiriporn nailed a 45-ft birdie putt on the 18th hole to tie Se Ri. Se Ri needed to par to force an 18-hole play-off. She made par under pressure to send it to an extra 18 holes.

Chuasiriporn started off strong, nailing a 30-ft birdie chip on the first hole. She grabbed a four-stroke lead heading into the 6th hole. Se Ri edged back into contention and then surged into the lead by making three birdies in 4 holes on the back 9. However, she bogeyed the 15th, and the two play-ers battled to a virtual standstill after 18 holes. This meant that the two had to play sudden-death. The pressure mounted, and perhaps, this was where her father's unorthodox training methods helped Se Ri. She drilled an 18-ft birdie putt on the second sudden-death hole to win the tournament. After 94 holes of golf, she had finally emerged victorious. "I really had a sixth sense she was going to make hers," Chuasiriporn said.[12]

A key to her success was her unflappability, her being seemingly imper-vious to nervousness. "No-ooo, I'm never nervous," when asked about nerves in 1998. "I never think of the crowd or the other players. I just play my game."[13]

Her amazing run in 1998 garnered praise from the game's greats. The world's number one player, Annika Sorenstam, said: "What she's done is incredible. And I'm glad for her because we need new faces."[14] "What she's doing has drawn more attention to women's golf than anything in a long, long time," said LPGA great Betsy Rawls. "I can't remember anything since Nancy Lopez that had this kind of impact. It thrills me to death."[15] She did much more than breathe new excitement to the women's tour; she inspired a nation. Prime Minister Kim Jong Pil said: "By winning four tournaments at a time that the nation was suffering difficult times, Pak encouraged the Korean people to have confidence that they can overcome any crisis."[16]

Se Ri added another victory at a major when she won the 2001 British Open by carding a final-round 66 to win by two strokes over fellow South Korean golfer Mi Hyun Kim. She had entered the final round four strokes behind but unveiled her patented "Pak Attack" on the back 9.

In 2002, Se Ri unveiled a "Pak attack" at the Betsy King Classic in Kutz-town, Pennsylvania. Entering the final round down by two strokes, Pak birdied the final 4 holes for course-record 63 and her sixteenth career title. Later that year she won her fourth career major title by winning her second LPGA Championship. One newspaper from Australia began their report by acknowledging that perennial greats Annika Sorenstam and Karrie Webb had to deal with a third superstar golfer: "If there was any lingering doubt, Se Ri Pak's second LPGA Championship victory in Delaware yesterday con-firmed that the Big Two of women's golf has expanded to include a third member."[17] She overcame a four-stroke deficit to win by three strokes over third-round leader Beth Daniel, who was seeking to become the oldest major winner in LPGA history. "What a lousy day," Daniel said. "I think the ghost of Babe Zaharias stepped on my ball."[18] The Babe had won the 1954 U.S. Women's Open at the age of 42 years, 11 months.

In 2005, Se Ri did not win a single tour event, plagued by a series of injuries to her finger, back, neck, and shoulder. She also suffered from a self-described case of burnout. However, she dug deep into her mental reservoir, assisted by an influx of Taekwondo and Thai boxing. She surprised the golfing world with her performance at the 2006 LPGA Championship in Havre de Grace, Maryland. She began the final round two strokes off the pace. She caught the leaders with a final-round 69 and ended up in a play-off with Karrie Webb, a seven-time major winner. On the first play-off hole, Se Ri hit a four-iron shot from more than 200 yards within 3 in. of the cup. The amazing shot garnered her third LPGA Championship and her fifth major. "I'm very happy to be back again," she said.[19]

Her place amongst the game's elite is unquestioned. "Se Ri is one of the three best women golfers of the last ten years, no question," says Eric Fleming, editor of the Web site SeoulSisters.com, a site devoted to the great South Korean female golfers. "She, Karrie Webb and Annika Sorenstam have accomplished far more than any other golfer you can name during that span, and deservedly have all qualified for the Hall of Fame."

Leading a Wave of Other Players

Se Ri's successes on the LPGA tour inspired a wave of other South Korean stars who have burst upon the scene. For this reason, some experts believe she has had as great as or greater impact than any golfer in the world today. "No other golfer has been more instrumental in affecting the very makeup of her sport," Fleming says. "Se Ri is literally the primary reason the LPGA went from having no Koreans in the mid 90s to over 40 today. Think of another sport where such a huge change has happened so quickly, let alone one where it can all be traced to the impact of one player."[20]

Fleming makes a solid case for Pak's impact in the world of golf. In 1997, there were no South Korean golfers on the LPGA tour. In Se Ri's rookie season in 1998, there were only three—including herself. By 2006, there were thirty-two South Koreans on the LPGA tour. "My success gave them confidence—they can play well too," Pak says. "When you come to the LPGA Tour, you can lead an entirely different life. It's not an easy adjustment, but they do it well."[21]

Some of the other South Korean golfers who followed Pak and have made a serious impact on the LPGA tour include Mi Hyun Kim, Grace Park, Hee-Won Han, Shi Hyun Ahn, Jeong Jang, Soo Yun Kang, Christina Kim, Meena Lee, Seon Hwa Lee, and Gloria Park.

Mi Hyun Kim stands only 5-foot-1 and weighs barely more than 100 pounds. But she has won eight LPGA tournaments and a second-place finish in the 2001 British Open. Grace Park has won six LPGA tournaments, including the 2004 Kraft Nabisco Championship. Hee-Won Han, who started on the LPGA tour in 2001, has won five LPGA tournaments, including Rookie of the Year honors. Shi Hyun Ahn won Rookie of the Year honors in 2004, won one tournament, and finished second at the 2004 LPGA Championship. Jeong Jang won the 2005 British Open for one of her two LPGA tournament wins. At the 2005 British Open, Jang led wire-to-wire, posting a 16-under par score to win by four strokes over Sophie Gustafon. Gloria Park, Christina Kim, and Meena Lee each have won two LPGA tournaments. Soo-Yun Kang and Seon Hwa Lee each have won an LPGA tournament.

Her fellow golfers honored Se Ri in 2006 with the prestigious Heather Farr Award, named after Heather Farr—an LPGA player who died in November 1993 after a battle with breast cancer. The award honors the LPGA player "who, through her hard work, dedication and love of the game of golf, has demonstrated determination, perseverance and spirit in fulfilling her goals as a player."[22] Se Ri was overjoyed at the award, saying: "Of all of my successes for nine years, this award is the most important and biggest, maybe for the rest of my life."[23]

"Besides her talent, drive, and accomplishments, she also has lived with more pressure than perhaps any other golfer in the world, male or female," Fleming says.

The pressure on her from the Korean fans, sponsors and media was so intense that she required hospitalization by the end of her rookie year on tour. Even then, the media barged into her hospital room and filmed her hooked up to an IV, crying. Yet despite all that, despite the occasional severe slumps and some debilitating injuries, she has time and again risen to the occasion and produced more wins, more top finishes, more Major victories. That's the mark of a true champion.[24]

A Trend of South Korean Golfers

The interesting question remains why have there been so many great Korean female golfers. Mi Hyun Kim calls it a "trend," adding: "Korean women are good at delicate sports like shooting and archery—good concentration. I don't know about American players, but we just try to practice very hard."[25] There is not a comparable development at all in the men's game. "The media over here always talks about the Korean junior program, but as far as I've been able to discover, there isn't such a thing," says Fleming.

In fact, it is actually very difficult to get onto golf courses in Korea. There are relatively few courses, and most of them are private. The membership fees for private courses are astronomical. Many Korean girls learn the game by playing on the ubiquitous driving ranges over there and get little experience on actual courses. It's one of the things that makes their success all the more remarkable.

Fleming says there really isn't a great junior program. "So, if there isn't a junior program, how is it there are so many great Korean junior golfers? And why women, but not men? There are many theories," Fleming says.

I think it's a combination of factors: women's golf is not so dependent on strength and driving distance as men's golf is, so the smaller Korean players are able to compete on the world stage (not that they are all small, but some of the best Korean golfers are). Golf is a game where hard work pays off, and nobody is willing to work as hard as the Koreans do. The Korean culture not only values hard work, they especially like to focus all that work in one specific area, which is why they excel in sports like archery, which also rewards intense, and focused, training. The culture also frowns upon huge displays of emotion, and golf seems to reward players who can remain calm even when things go against them. These are all factors that make a difference, but in my opinion, the biggest factor is without a doubt the work ethic. It's amazing how many hours these ladies put in to be the best.[26]

Successful South Koreans living in the United States confirm that the Korean culture at least partly contributes to this incredible striving for greater achievement seen in Se Ri Pak and other Korean golfers. "Many kids in Korea face tremendous pressure from their parents to succeed," says David H. Kim, a highly successful radiation oncologist living in Evansville, Indiana. "Whatever they do, they have to be the best at it. This may be one of the roots as to why Pak is as determined and driven as she is to succeed."[27] His wife Doris Kim, formerly Young Shin Pak (no relation to the golfer), agrees, stating: "In Korean culture, the goal is to succeed and the way to be successful is to be single-minded, hardworking and have a strong belief in personal responsibility. These values are stressed at a very young age."[28]

Doris Kim offers an intriguing possibility as to why there have been so many successful Korean golfers to follow Se Ri Pak. "In New York City, when I lived there, I observed that some Korean immigrants would open up their own business and by being very hardworking, they would succeed. Then, after a short period of time, there would be another Korean-owned store right across the street in the same area." She explains that the same phenomenon may have happened with respect to other golfers following Se Ri Pak. "There is a culture of competition," she says, "measuring your work in comparison to others."[29] She notes that this may not explain every golfer from South Korea, as "people are different." Doris, a deep thinker, explains that perhaps Se Ri Pak may simply "love excelling at her sport and be very much in competition with herself and believe that by overcoming fear you are evolving as a human being. To some, overcoming fear and evolving toward more excellence is a real high."[30]

Whatever the root cause of the incredible South Korean influence on the LPGA, Fleming believes that the global expansion of the women's game and the LPGA will only continue. "China is only starting to enter the golf world, but with more than a billion people, you have to believe they will produce some world class talent in the future. Lorena Ochoa will doubtless inspire Mexicans and other Central and South Americans, and in the past few years there have been several other promising players coming from that area of the world [including Julieta Granada, a Paraguayan who won the ADT Championship in 2006, and Angela Park, a Korean-Brazilian who is leading the LPGA's rookie of the year race so far this year (she has five top-ten finishes in 2007)]. There is every indication that this trend will continue."[31]

—— CHAPTER 11 ——

POTENTIAL GREAT

There is another golfer with South Korean roots who could be better than Se Ri Pak and everyone else in the world. She qualified for an LPGA event at the age of twelve. She won the U.S. Women's Amateur Championship at the age of thirteen. She played an LPGA major championship—the Kraft Nabisco Championship—was in serious contention. She missed a 2004 PGA tour event by only one stroke when she was 14 years old. She stands 6-foot-1 and can drive the ball more than 300 yards. She has unlimited potential but is yet to actually win an LPGA tournament event, although, surely, that can only be a matter of time. She is the one and only Michelle Wie.

Wie possesses all the physical tools, as evidenced by her shooting 68 at the PGA tour event. She is a prodigy of prodigies, having been playing the sport in her home state of Hawaii since she was only 4 years old. She got her golfing genes honestly, as her father Byung Wook Kim has a 2-handicap and her mother Hyun Kyong was an amateur champion back in South Korea.[1] She began walking at the age of nine.[2] She took to the game like a fish to water, beating her parents by the time she was only 8 years old. The next year she broke par for the first time. Most golfers never break par, but Wie did when she was only 9 years old.

She also worked very hard to improve her game constantly. Author Jennifer Mario explains: "Michelle's willingness to put in the long hours may have had something to do with her upbringing. She was, after all, raised by two Korean parents, and they raised her with Korean values—specifically, they taught her that, first, success comes only with hard work and, second, education is paramount."[3]

She was never afraid to play with older women or men. She played against men at the Manoa Cup Hawaii State Amateur Match-Play championship, becoming the youngest person and first woman to qualify in 2001. She won a match in the event the next year.[4]

In 2003, Wie stepped up her game and accomplishments in a major way. She played in the LPGA 2003 Kraft Nabisco tournament and finished in the top ten (at ninth). Later that year she won the U.S. Women's Amateur Public Links tournament. She triumphed in the match-play tournament with a 1-hole victory over Virada Nirapathpongporn, the winner of the NCAA championships from Duke. Wie won the 36th and final hole with her superior driving ability. "I think it will probably be one of the most memorable matches I've played," the gracious Nirapathpongporn said. "Michelle put on a great show. I really enjoyed it; I came out one shot short. But it was great playing with her. She's everything everyone talked about."[5]

In 2005 Wie finished second at the SBS Open at the Turtle Bay Resort, finishing only two shots behind winner Jennifer Rosales. Later in the year she finished second to the great Annika Sorenstam at the Kraft Nabisco Championship. Then, at the U.S. Open she found herself in a tie for the lead after the third round. Unfortunately, she had a bad final round that left her in a tie with, ironically, Sorenstam in twenty-third place.

She continued to face criticism from other women professionals who criticized her receiving sponsor exemptions into tournaments and then trying to play with the men before she had won an LPGA event. She also received criticism from male players for her playing PGA tour events. Wie responded with a written letter to the Associated Press that explains her position forcefully and clearly:

This is Michelle Wie. I would like to take this opportunity to clarify myself with regards to playing in professional events and not following the conventional path that many great golfers have gone through.…

People always ask why I do what I do and why not just follow the conventional path. My answer is very simple. I always wanted to push myself to the limit. I started walking when I was nine months old and I started reading when I was just over one year old and I started reading when I was just over a year old. I started playing golf when I was 4 and shot a 64 when I was 10. I was not only a girl on the boys' baseball team but also the best hitter. I qualified for the WAPL when I was 10 years old and made the cut. I always wanted to do things fast. I always wanted to be the first and youngest to do things.

I feel grateful for all the sponsor exemptions that the tournaments have offered to me. I cherish each and every one of them.…A lot of people criticize my choice to play in the PGA Tour events, but I am really happy to be there. I get to know the players and get to play a PGA Tour course. It's really fun and I think it helps me to get ready or my ultimate goal of becoming a PGA Tour member. I am not afraid of failure, and I cannot be. When I went to the Great Wall of China, I was really excited. I was walking up the stairs and going really high. I got tired and looked down. At that point I saw how high I was and what would happen if I fell.

I am not going to do whatever the critics want me to do because they always change their minds anyway. No matter what the critics say about me, I am going to do whatever my heart tells me to do and I thank my parents for always backing me up. Dream big and I will reach the sky; dream small and my feet will never get off the ground.[6]

She continued to dream big and go for the gusto. In 2005, she nearly qualified for the prestigious Masters tournament at Augusta National for the PGA. She entered the U.S. Amateur Publinx male tournament and won three matches before falling to eventual winner Clay Ogden. She then placed third in the Women's British Open. After opening with a 75, she followed that up with successive rounds of 67, 67, and 69. "The year 2005 was one in which Michelle really couldn't complain. She played in three men's and eight LPGA events and had four top-five finishes, including two in majors."[7]

Though she was disqualified from the 2005 World Samsung Open, unfairly according to many, for a bad drop, Wie continues to pursue her ultimate dream of playing on the PGA tour. Many believe that she will one day become a Tiger Woods of female golf, dominating the tour. The criticism from some golfers persists. U.S. Open winner Michael Campbell said in May 2006: "Michelle Wie is obviously a wonderful talent," he said. "She hits it as long as the guys. But she needs to prove to herself—more so than to anybody else—that she can win on the ladies tour before she can come out and actually make a cut on the U.S. Tour or the European Tour."[8]

Reporter Ian O'Connor wrote: "Let Wie earn her driver's license before casting her career as a wreck."[9]

Wie may not even be the best of the young female golfers. Amy Yang has played on the Ladies European Tour and won the tour's prestigious ANZ Ladies Master in Australia near where she lives with a sudden-death win over the great Karrie Webb. "She has the talent to win anywhere against any type of field," said the Australian Ladies Professional Golf general manager Warren Sevil. "She beat Karrie Webb at the ANZ Ladies Masters and look what Karrie's done this year."[10]

— CHAPTER 12 —

THE INTRACTABLE COLOR LINE

The national preference for white skin may define a problem that is beyond solution, absent a nation of the blind. Too many of our institutions are based on exclusion of some from the blessings and benefits of our systems and its society. This creates a sub-society that must take what it wants, alas.

—Judge Bruce Wright[1]

Of all the races and varieties of men which have suffered from this feeling, the colored people of this country have endured most. They can resort to no disguises which will enable them to escape its deadly aim. They carry in front the evidence which marks them for persecution. They stand at the extreme point of difference from the Caucasian race, and their African origin can be instantly recognized, though they may be several removes from the typical African race....They are Negroes—and that is enough, in the eye of this unreasoning prejudice, to justify indignity and violence. In nearly every department of American life they are confronted by this insidious influence. It fills the air. It meets them at the workshop and factory, when they apply for work. It meets them at the church, at the hotel, at the ballot-box, and worst of all, it meets them in the jury-box....He has escaped from the galleys, and hence all presumptions are against him. The workshop denies him work, and the inn denies him shelter; the ballot-box a fair vote, and the jury-box a fair trial. He has ceased to be the slave of an individual, but has in some sense become the slave of society. He may not now be bought and sold like a beast in the market, but he is the trammeled victim of a prejudice, well calculated to repress his manly ambition, paralyze his energies, and make him a dejected and spiritless man, if not a sullen enemy to society, fit to prey upon life and property and to make trouble generally.

—Frederick Douglass[2]

In his book *Two Nations,* Andrew Hacker wrote: "Race has been an American obsession since the first Europeans sighted 'savages' on these shores.... But race in America took on a deeper and more disturbing meaning with the importation of Africans as slaves.... Throughout this nation's history, race has always had a central role."[3] In 1903, the great African-American author W. E. B. Du Bois once wrote that the problem of the twentieth century is "the problem of the color line." In the words of a Harvard professor Cornel West, "Race Matters."[4] Unfortunately, race has mattered much in the sport of golf, particularly when it comes to the race that was enslaved in the United States of America since the first arrival of Africans to Jamestown in 1619.

Racism exists in many forms and fashions, but the virulence of racism directed toward African-Americans has been the harshest. In other words, as Hacker and others have noted, the greatest racial divide in the United States has been between whites and blacks. Randall Kennedy writes in his book *Race, Crime and the Law:* "This is the conflict that has served as the great object lesson for American law, the conflict that has given birth to much of the federal constitutional law of criminal procedure, and the conflict that remains the most pervasive and volatile point of racial friction within federal and state courthouses."[5]

African-Americans have been faced with a horrid history of discrimination in sport, as well as in other societal issues. Examine any sports and one can find evidence of severe discrimination, often through fixed rules of segregation. Jack Johnson became the first African-American world heavyweight boxing champion in 1908 and held his title until 1915 but faced the hatred of White America. Johnson faced the most virulent types of racism when he captured the world heavyweight championship in 1908. His historic victory over the former champion James J. Jeffries on July 4, 1910, started race riots and led to the banning of fight films.

Racism and Johnson's own obstreperous and outrageous conduct prevented any African-American from having another shot at a world title until Joe Louis in 1937.

Jackie Robinson did not break the color barrier in major league baseball until 1947. The reception he received from fans and even other players was downright despicable. Opponents would spike him as he slid into second base; fans would jeer him with the vilest of racial insults, and many places in the South denied him basic accommodations with his white teammates. The National Basketball Association—now dominated by African-Americans—was not integrated until 1950.

Tennis and golf were even more lily-white, partly because African-Americans were largely denied access to the best public facilities. Many public golf courses were segregated by law. Segregation laws had been sanctioned by the U.S. Supreme Court in its 1896 decision *Plessy v. Ferguson* when the Court upheld an 1890 Louisiana public accommodations law that provided for mandatory separate railway coaches for blacks and whites.[6] The case involved the 1892 arrest Homer Plessy, an octoroon—an offensive term for a person who was one-eight black—for boarding a whites-only coach. Rodolphe Desdunes, the leader of the New Orleans American Citizens' Equal Rights Association, had recruited his friend Plessy for the specific purpose of challenging the segregation law. Plessy and Desdunes took the case all the way to the U.S. Supreme Court.

In one of its most unfortunate decisions, the Court upheld the doctrine of separate and equal, meaning that it was not unconstitutional to provide for separate facilities based on race as long as they were substantially equal. Writing for the majority, Justice Henry Billings Brown reasoned:

We consider the underlying fallacy of the plaintiff's argument to consist in the assumption that the enforced separation of the two races stamps the colored race with a badge of inferiority....If the two races are to meet upon terms of social equality, it must be the result of each other's merits, and a voluntary consent of individuals....If one race be inferior to the other socially, the Constitution of the United States cannot put them on the same plane.

In other words, the U.S. Supreme Court gave legal sanction to the rank practice of discriminating against blacks by giving them separate (and unequal) facilities.

Only Justice John Marshall Harlan of Kentucky, a former slave owner, dissented in powerful and oft-cited language:

But in view of the constitution, in the eye of the law, there is in this country no superior, dominant ruling class of citizens. There is no caste here. Our constitution is color blind and neither knows nor tolerates classes among citizens. In respect of civil rights, all citizens are equal before the law. The humblest is the peer of the most powerful. The law regards man as man, and takes no account of his surroundings or of his color when his civil rights as guaranteed by the supreme law of the land are involved.

In part because of this decision, Harlan was known as "the Great Dissenter."

Unfortunately, the sad reality was that separate but equal normally meant separate and unequal in all facets of American life. States provided separate facilities for blacks but they were horribly inferior. In education many states far outspent for white schools than black schools. *Plessy v. Ferguson* ushered in a staunch period of segregation. The state of Alabama even had a law that prohibited whites and blacks from playing checkers together.

Change did not come, particularly in the South, until the U.S. Supreme Court issued its historic decision in 1954 in *Brown v. Board of Education*. In that decision, the Court ruled that segregation in public education violated the Equal Protection Clause of the Fourteenth Amendment. Chief

Justice Earl Warren wrote: "We conclude that in the field of public education the doctrine of 'separate but equal' has no place. Separate educational
facilities are inherently unequal."[7] The Court relied on social science studies
by Dr. Kenneth Clark, which showed that young black children favored
white dolls over black dolls.

The *Brown v. Board of Education* decision ushered in a new era of constitutional law, as courts invalidated various other segregation laws. The U.S.
Supreme Court desegregated restaurants and restrooms in *Turner v. City
of Memphis* (1962), interstate transportation facilities and carriers in *Bailey
v. Patterson* (1962), public parks in *Watson v. City of Memphis* (1963),
public parks in Georgia in *Evans v. Newton* (1966), and Alabama prisons
in *Lee v. Washington* (1968).

Lower federal courts in Louisiana and Texas struck down state laws that
prohibited interracial boxing matches. African-American boxers I.H.
"Sporty" Harvey and Joseph Dorsey successfully challenged state laws in
Texas and Louisiana banning interracial bouts. Other lower courts invalidated a host of laws that segregated public restrooms, swimming pools,
and restaurants.

THE RACE BARRIER IN GOLF

> If one sport has embodied deep-rooted racial prejudice, it is this one, on both
> the amateur and professional levels. African Americans have excluded from
> golf since its inception in the country, and the game is now in the 1990's recov-
> ering from the ravages of its history.
>
> —Jim Gullo[8]

> A private golf club, however, restricted to either Negro or white membership is
> one expression of freedom of association. But a municipal golf course that
> serves only one race is state activity indicating a preference on a matter as to
> which the State must be neutral.
>
> —Justice William O. Douglas[9]

> Racism has been an undeniable part of golf's history.
>
> —Clifton Brown[10]

The only place that blacks had for many years in the game of golf was as
caddies. The PGA did not officially desegregate until 1961, when it removed
its pernicious whites-only clause. There were positive moments in history but
they were all too fleeting. In 1896 African-American golfer John Shippen, a
caddie at Shinnecock Hills on Long Island, played in the second U.S. Open
at the Shinnecock Hills Golf Club. When other players complained about
Shippen and a Native American golfer, the USGA (United States Golf Association) stood firm. Theodore F. Havemeyer said: "We're going to play this

thing today even if Shippen and Bunn [the Native American golfer] are the only people in it."[11] Havemeyer alleging told those golfers who threatened a boycott: "We'll miss you but Mr. Shippen plays."[12] Shippen finished fifth. In 1939, the Canadian Open was delayed more than 30 minutes when officials were faced with a potential crisis when an African-American player showed up with an approved entry to play. The officials scrambled to find a player that would play with the African-American. Jug McSpaden volunteered, and as Shirley Povich wrote: "Jug McSpaden volunteered and justice of some kind was served. McSpaden [whose real first name was Harold] went on to win the tournament."[13] Shippen also played in several more U.S. Opens in 1899, 1900, 1902, and 1913. Shippen may have won the 1896 Open and perhaps changed the course of race in golf if he had not carded a disastrous 11 on the 13th hole. He recounted in an interview in 1967, the year before his death:

It was a little, easy par four. I'd played it many times and I knew I just had to stay on the right side of the fairway with my drive. Well, I played it too far to the right and the ball landed in a sand road. Bad trouble in those days before sand wedges. I kept hitting the ball along the road, unable to lift it out of the sand, and wound up with an unbelievable eleven for the hole. You know, I've wished a hundred times I could have played that little par four again. It sure would have been something to win that day.[14]

Around the turn of the century, George F. Grant, an African-American dentist, patented the first golf tee. He played in the Boston suburb of Arlington Heights with several friends. He became frustrated with having to use molds of sand to create a tee for his golf shots. He thought of the idea of using small wooden pegs to support the ball when he hit it. In December 1899, he received a patent from the United States Patent Office for his golf tee—the first one registered in the country. He had a small shop manufacture the tees but he never sought a commercial profit for his design. Years later a white golfer, ironically also a dentist, received a patent for his golf tee and he made money off his invention. The white dentist, Dr. William Lowell, was considered the inventor of the golf tee for many years. Finally in 1991, the USGA recognized Dr. Grant as the first person to patent a golf tee.[15]

African-American golfers were forced to play among themselves. In 1928, male players banded together and formed the UGA (United Golf Association). The UGA featured some star players, including Charlie Sifford and Ted Rhodes. Rhodes won well over a hundred tournaments in the UGA but never got a chance to play on the PGA tour. Sifford finally broke the color barrier in the 1960s but he was already 37 years old. He still managed to win twice on the PGA tour, including a victory at the 1969 Los Angeles Open when he was forty-six.

The PGA itself contributed to this legacy of discrimination. In 1943 it adopted a provision to its bylaws that provided that only "professional golfers of the Caucasian Race...shall be eligible for membership." This bylaw was the law of the PGA for nearly 20 years. By contrast, the LPGA since its inception in 1950 has never had such a blatant provision of discrimination. When the Shoal Creek controversy surfaced, the LPGA commissioner William Blue pointed out that the LPGA works diligently to ensure that no clubs sponsoring tournaments are discriminatory. "This association stands for golf for everyone," he said. "After all, we are an association of women, who often have been discriminated against by club restrictions."[16]

Segregation was the way of life in many parts of the country. This meant that blacks could not play on many city golf courses. They were relegated to inferior courses or nothing at all. Many times African-American golfers were relegated to 9-hole courses, while white golfers had their pick of multiple 18-hole courses. That was the case in the city of Baltimore, Maryland, until NAACP head Charles Houston litigated a case on behalf of Mr. Law, a black man who petitioned city officials to allow him access to play on one of the city's three whites-only golf courses. The city maintained four golf courses—three for whites and one for blacks. The course for blacks was only 9 holes, while the three for whites were all 18 holes. In 1948, a federal district court judge ruled that the city failed to provide substantially equal facilities for blacks. The judge reasoned:

But in many other respects the white courses are greatly superior to the Carroll Park course, which is only a 9-hole course while all the others are of 18 holes. For an experienced golfer with reasonably vigorous physical activity, it is difficult to say that a 9-hole golf course is of substantial equality with an 18-hole course, if other qualities are otherwise fairly comparable. One of the pleasurable features of golf consists in the variety of the type of play afforded by varied conditions of ground on an 18-hole course. Most golfers desire to play at least 18 holes at one time.[17]

Five citizens in Houston, Texas, sued the city after being denied admission to the municipal golf facility. The five plaintiffs sued in federal court, contending that city officials had violated their equal-protection rights under the Fourteenth Amendment. A federal district judge rejected their claim, writing: "I do not think the failure to provide golf courses in parks used by negroes is, either as a matter of law or fact, a discrimination against negroes."

The plaintiffs appealed to the fifth U.S. Circuit Court of Appeals—a federal appeals court composed of some very fair and courageous federal judges, including John Minor Wisdom, Elbert Tuttle, and others. The fifth Circuit reversed the lower court and found that the city of Houston had violated the plaintiffs' constitutional rights:

In thus holding, the district judge erred in fact and in law. He erred in fact because, if an individual negro citizen desires to play golf on a municipal course and is prevented from doing so only because he is a negro citizen, while an individual white citizen, because he is not a negro, is permitted to do so, the fact that he is being discriminated against in the assertion of a personal and individual right, because of his color, stands out like a sore thumb, or like a large blob on the end of a small nose.

He erred in law because his conclusion is contrary to the general principles established by the authorities.... What was accomplished here under the purported sanction of state law is the very thing the Constitution was written to make impossible, and the civil rights statutes forbid. That is denying to a negro, because he is a negro, his individual, his personal, right as a citizen to use and enjoy a facility furnished at the public expense while permitting a white man, because he is white, to use and enjoy it.[18]

Despite these rulings, many cities continued to discriminate against African-American golfers. It took further litigation to firmly establish that such discrimination was flatly unconstitutional.

RACIAL DISCRIMINATION AT THE CLUB LEVEL

The race factor played a role in golf at the country club level. Most infamously, the issue came to the forefront of the American consciousness in 1990 on the eve of the PGA Championships, which was to be held at Shoal Creek Country Club in Birmingham, Alabama. When interviewed about his club's membership policies and other issues, the club president Hall Thompson stated: "We have the right to associate or not to associate with whomever we choose. The country club is our home and we pick and choose who we want. I think we've said we don't discriminate in every other are except the blacks."[19]

Public reaction was swift from the media, which called for end to the flagrant discrimination based on race. "Shoal Creek" became synonymous with discrimination. Organizations threatened to picket outside the Birmingham club's grounds. Sponsors yanked millions of commercial dollars from the television networks. The club quickly agreed to allow an African-American to join the club. Thirteen years later in 2003, the club had six members.[20]

In response, the PGA and LPGA amended their policies to prohibit the hosting of any tournament by a club that discriminated on the basis of race, sex, religion, or national origin. Most clubs complied by opening their membership ranks at least to some degree. A few—about ten—voluntarily gave up their affiliation with a professional golf tournament to keep their policies of exclusion.

Shoal Creek may have received the most media attention but it was not an isolated incident in American history. As one legal commentator noted: "discrimination against racial minorities and women is a deep seated tradition in American country clubs."[21]

In 1969, Washington DC mayor Walter Washington was barred from speaking at a women's group at Kenwood Country Club in Bethesda, Maryland.[22] A black golfer did not play The Masters at the fabled Augusta National until Lee Elder qualified in 1975. Two years earlier, the *Washington Post* wrote that "Elder was more at home in apartheid Johannesburg (South Africa) than magnolia Augusta."[23]

In 1984, the Loudoun Golf and Country Club in Loudoun, Virginia, settled a racial discrimination suit brought by former member Norman Green and his would-be visitor Arthur Brown. In 1982, club officials allegedly ordered Brown off the premises because of his race. The confidential settlement included some monies paid to the two African-American men and the club's agreement to adopt a nondiscrimination clause in its policy.[24]

In 1985, former NFL defensive end Sherman White alleged that no one would sponsor his membership to the Sequoyah Country Club in Oakland, California. White pointed out the irony: "These are people who've rooted for me.... But they wouldn't get behind me and let me in."[25]

ANN GREGORY—THE FIRST GREAT AFRICAN-AMERICAN FEMALE GOLFER

Many histories of golf don't mention the name of Ann Moore-Gregory. If society had been more equitable in her day and age, her name would be common knowledge. She was the finest African-American female golfer of her generation—sometimes called "the Queen of Negro Women's Golf"—but segregation prevented her from showcasing her skills on the highest stages.[26]

Born in Aberdeen, Mississippi, in July 1912, Ann Moore and her family moved to Gary, Indiana, where she played tennis. Her husband Percy Gregory played golf so much that she considered divorcing him. However, after he went away to fight in World War II, she took the game in part because she missed him dearly. She also caught the golf bug for the rest of her life.[27]

She dominated black golfing tournaments sponsored by the UGA. Dr. Calvin Sinnette, a golf historian who has written extensively on African-Americans in golf, writes: "During the next half-decade, Ann Gregory was such a dominant force in African-American women's golf that some of her competitors asked for a handicap."[28]

In September 1956, she participated in the U.S. Women's Amateur Championship at Meridian Hills Country Club in Indianapolis, becoming the first African-American woman to play in a national championship conducted by the USGA. At the U.S. Women's Amateur tournament in Williamstown, Massachusetts, the players were staying together at a hotel. One of the competitors saw Gregory, mistook her for a maid and asked her for a hanger. Gregory complied by bringing a hanger and laughed over the incident with the fellow competitor.

Other incidents of a racial nature were no laughing matter. In 1959, she was excluded from a players' dinner because the social tour-site host discriminated on the basis of race. In the early 1960s, she successfully challenged the city of Gary, Indiana, policy of race and golf. The black golfers were restricted to a 9-hole course, while white golfers could play the 18-hole courses. Gregory boldly paid her fee and played her round at the 18-hole course without incident. Her brave action caused the city to change its policy.

She played in numerous national USGA events over the years. In 1971, she lost by one stroke to Carolyn Cudone at the USGA Senior Women's Amateur at Sea Island Golf Club. Her golfing career culminated with a gold medal in the Senior Olympic Games in 1989. At the age of seventy-six, Gregory beat everyone else in the field, which included women in the fifties. She fired a 75 and 79 to win her gold medal. She died the following year in February 1990 at the age of seventy-seven.

In 1999, the *Orlando Sentinel* listed the fifty most influential women of the twentieth century. Ann Moore-Gregory ranked number eighteen.[29]

"She was a determined and confident golfer," said Renee Powell, the second African-American to play on the LPGA tour, "and she was such a warm-hearted, inspirational individual that she helped me by her example, by the kind of person she was. She set the stage for every other black female who came into golf after her."[30]

A LEGEND BREAKS THE COLOR BARRIER

A familiar face finally broke the color barrier in the LPGA—tennis champion Althea Gibson. She amazed the tennis world when in 1957 and 1958 she won Wimbledon and the U.S. Open. She captured her first title at the age of thirty by defeating Darlene Hard. In those days, Wimbledon and the U.S. Open were reserved for amateur players. After 1958, Gibson turned professional and never competed in tennis' major championships again.

Born in Silver, South Carolina, Gibson was the daughter of a sharecropper and cotton farmer. She left South Carolina at the age of three and moved to Harlem, New York. There, she turned her attention to golf. She excelled at all sports, particularly basketball. She played 4 years of varsity basketball in college and 3 years collegiately at Florida Agricultural and Mechanical College (Florida A&M), where she majored in health and physical education. She got the golf bug in 1959 after a friend took her to play at the Inglewood Country Club in New Jersey. She had played at Florida A&M but never thought she would ever play professionally, as tennis was her primary focus. After the trip to Inglewood Country Club, she devoted her post-tennis life to become the best golfer she could be.

In 1961, she announced that she would try her hand as a golf professional. She wished to duplicate her grand tennis success on the links by becoming a golf champion. The odds were against her, as she picked up the game so late in life. Unlike tennis, which she played as a youngster, she took up golf past her athletic prime. Gibson recognized the challenges, saying she would start slowly. "I don't plan to play in major tournaments until I believe I can win—or at least be a good challenger," she said. "So far I've been pleased with my progress. I've been playing golf for less than two years and only shot six rounds last year. I've had a low of an 84."[31]

Gibson took her task seriously, following the LPGA women on tour. She talked golf with Louise Suggs, Marilyn Smith, Marlene Bauer Hagge, and other top players. She possessed the ability to hit very long drives and putted pretty well. Her weaknesses, according to her, were with her irons.

She showed some promise early in her golfing career by winning the Yorkshire-Dandy Duffers tournament in Pittsburgh, Pennsylvania—a United States Golfers Association link's tournament in July 1961. She shot a 79 her first round and a 95 in the second round but still won the tournament by thirteen strokes. The 79 was Gibson's lowest competitive round of golf ever.[32]

She dominated the annual North-South Negro golf tournament for black golfers. In February 1962, she won the tournament, which was held in Miami, holding a lead at one by time by a whopping twenty strokes. In August 1962, she entered her first Women's National Amateur Golf title, an event that featured the country's best amateur players in a match-play format. Gibson lost 2-up to Mrs. Paul Dye of Indianapolis. Gibson had a 2-hole advantage after 9 holes, but slipped down the stretch.[33] In July 1963, she repeated as champion of the North-South Negro tournament, winning by an incredible thirty-six strokes. The *Chicago Defender* proclaimed that she was on the "verge of new success in the world of sports."[34]

Later that year Gibson qualified for the LPGA at the age of thirty-six—the first African-American to play in the LPGA. Gibson encountered racism on the tour—not from the LPGA officials but from some places where the tour played. Lennie Wirtz, the LPGA tournament director in the 1960s, told Liz Kahn:

I remember going into a restaurant with her, and the waiter wouldn't come to our table and serve us. I told her not to make a scene, and we walked out. There was also a golf club where they said Althea could play the course, but they didn't want her to use the john or the locker room. We got a new sponsor and venue for that date.[35]

Fellow LPGA player Marlene Hagge, who roomed for Gibson sometimes on the road, told Kahn: "We had trouble, especially in the South, and we said we wouldn't play unless Althea could be treated like everyone else. I'm proud of the LPGA and what we did."[36]

Gibson endured these insults and tried her best at golf at the highest level. She failed to make the cut in the six events she played in 1963. She requalified in 1964 and remained a fixture on tour for the rest of the 1960s and into the 1970s. Gibson had her moments of greatness but never won an LPGA event.

In August 1966, she shot an opening round 68 in the Lady Carling golf tournament at the Pleasant Valley Country Club in Sutton, Massachusetts. Gibson's 68 broke the course record held by the great Mickey Wright. It was one of those days where Gibson backed up her long drives with excellent putting and short-iron play. The United Press International reported that she "used her short irons and putter with near textbook perfection on the back nine."[37] No one else that round did better than a 72. Unfortunately, she dropped off dramatically after her fast start, carding an 88 in her second round. At one hole, her shot careened off a spectator's pocketbook and landed in the water.[38] She shot a final-round 80 and finished a distant twenty-fourth, while the tournament was won by Kathy Whitworth—the LPGA's all-time tournament winner.

Gibson recognized the tough hurdles as she was into her golfing career: "I've only been playing golf since 1959. What do you expect in eight years, especially against players who have been playing since they were 12 or 13."[39]

In 1968, Gibson at the age of forty-one even attempted a comeback in her best sport tennis. The Associated Press reported her tennis comeback, noting that she was a "former tennis queen but just a commoner among women's professional golfers."[40] Gibson said: "Tennis is my first love and that's where the money is."[41]

From 1963 to 1977, Gibson played in 171 PGA tournaments without ever winning. She came close on several occasions, cracking the top ten in several tournaments. She finished tied for third at one event in 1967, finished sixth in one event in 1968, and tied for the second in 1970. She may have never won an LPGA tournament but she won far more—she broke the color barrier. "Althea was the Jackie Robinson for Black women in professional golf," says professor Dana Brooks. "This year we celebrated the 60th birthday of Jack's integration of professional baseball in America. We should also take time to celebrate the efforts and contributions of Althea Gibson to the sports of golf and tennis in America."[42]

In 1980, the Women's Sports Hall of Fame inducted its inaugural class of nine women. That class included Patty Berg, Babe Didrikson Zaharias, and Althea Gibson.

She died in September 2003 at the age of seventy-six. The great golf writer Rhonda Glenn summed it up best:

While the athleticism was there, she was so new to the game, and so raw, that she never came close to achieving what she had in tennis. Gibson, however, had the courage to tee it up in public despite her lack of experience and training. She entered the arena and it's Gibson's striving that we celebrate today.[43]

RENEE POWELL

Renee Powell became the second African-American player to join the LPGA tour in 1967. She played until 1977, competing in more than 250 LPGA tournaments. Powell got an early start in the game of golf when her father William handed her a sawed-off putter and junior-sized driver.

She had access to golf because her father built his own golf course in East Canton, Ohio, so that blacks could play golf regularly rather than face discrimination from government officials. Renee graduated high school in 1964 and played at both Ohio University and Ohio State University. She joined the tour in 1967, which was her father's proudest moment.

Powell experienced racism while playing on the Tour, though noting that Gibson had paved the way and encountered more problems. She received life-threatening letters. "I became very paranoid," she told the *New York Times*. "I thought someone was going to jump out from behind a tree or something. I thought about getting a gun but I never did. Nothing ever happened, other than some obscene phone calls. That's the only time I ever ran into anything as a professional golfer."[44]

The incidents though made her appreciate golf in Europe more than the United States. "I find I enjoy and appreciate playing in Europe because I have a greater sense of freedom," she told the *Los Angeles Times*. "It makes me sad to say that. I really love my country."[45]

Powell hoped that her playing efforts would cause other African-Americans to take to the game. She wanted to win tournaments so that "black kids watching television would be inspired to try and learn to golf."[46]

Like Gibson, Powell never won an LPGA tournament. She finished in the top ten thrice, including a fourth-place finish. Yet, she was a winner, as she—like Althea Gibson—made history for her trailblazing ways.

LAREE SUGG

The third African-American female to play on tour was LaRee Pearl Sugg, a former all-American player at UCLA, whom she led to the 1991 NCAA championship. Sugg played on the LPGA for several years, including 1995, 1996, 2000, and 2001. She qualified for six U.S. Opens and four British Opens. She won titles on the lower futures tour at the 1998 Aurora Health Futures Classic. She finished eighth at one LPGA event—the 2000 Wegman's Rochester International. Sugg's grandfather introduced her to the game at the age of six. She won more than thirty junior titles in her career before earning the Amy Alcott Scholarship at UCLA.

In March 2002, The University of Richmond hired Sugg to coach their first women's golf team. She currently serves in the school's athletic department as the Assistant Director of Athletics/Senior Woman Administrator.

In that capacity, she still qualified for the 2006 U.S. Open—an amazing accomplishment for a part-time player.[47]

FUTURE PLAYERS

There remains a paucity of African-American players in the women's game. The *Richmond Times Dispatch* quoted an unnamed LPGA official as saying: "If you're black and you're a woman, it's almost as though you start with two strikes against you."[48] However, there are no official barriers that blocked Ann Moore-Gregory. The LPGA welcomes players from all races, nationalities, and backgrounds as long as they shoot a low enough score. Andia Winslow, the cousin of former San Diego Chargers all-pro Kellen Winslow, competed at the Ginns Club and Resorts Open in Reunion, Florida, as an amateur golfer with a sponsor's exemption. She missed the cut but remains hopeful for the future.

WHY SO FEW?

There are many possible reasons for the lack of African-Americans on the LPGA and the PGA too for that matter. One is the question of access. Golf remains a sport dominated by the country club elite, and for many years African-Americans were excluded by and large either by economics or by racial discrimination. Obviously, improvements have been made but it will take time for that to filter down to young competitors.

There may be other causes. Writer Gwen Daye Richardson reasons: "Because blacks were barred so long, legally or in practice, from the nation's elite sports, we're generally not real interested in watching or participating in such games as long as all of the prominent faces remain white."[49] Another factor remains access to golf—a sport that has long been the province of the exclusive. Dwight Lewis, a prominent African-American editorial columnist for the *Tennessean*, makes the point: "I'm 59 years old and when I was younger, there simply weren't places to play."[50]

A *USA TODAY* poll of African-Americans revealed some possible solutions to attract that segment of the population to the sport. The suggestions included "more teaching" in the form of clinics and youth programs, lowering the cost of the sport and more publicizing of the sport.[51]

The popularity of Tiger Woods, whose late father, Earl, was African-American, has increased greater participation of African-Americans. Woods himself sees the potential for greater diversity, as he sees persons of color in galleries and junior golf tournaments. "I think the game has certainly evolved, certainly grown and become more diverse. There is no doubt about that," Woods said. "Look at our galleries (on tour) and they've changed quite a bit. Junior golf programs around the country that I've seen certainly have more diversity."[52]

However, even in 2007 there are virtually no African-American golfers on the PGA or LPGA tours. "There's not been an appropriate bridge developed for those young people who have the talent and interest from diverse backgrounds to give them the opportunity [to receive] the finest, best teaching methods in order to understand if they have the skill and desire to go on," said Joe Louis Barrow Jr. (the son of former heavyweight champion Joe Louis), the executive director of First Tee. "That is a void in what has occurred in the last several years."[53]

"I'm a little surprised by that," said golfing great Annika Sorenstam in reference to the lack of African-Americans on the LPGA tour. "I don't know why. You look at tennis and wow—they're phenomenal. One of these days, they'll pick up a golf club and then you'll see them here."[54]

Hopefully, Sorenstam is right and you will see more African-American faces on the LPGA tour.

—— Chapter 13 ——

Gender Discrimination

As insidious as racial discrimination has been, so has gender discrimination. Sadly, the Declaration of Independence only says "All men are created equal" instead of "all people." Women did not receive the right to vote in the United States until the ratification of the Nineteenth Amendment in 1920. They were treated like second-class citizens. It took the actions of women suffragists taking to the streets as "rampant women" to force society to take notice of the inequities in women not being able to exercise the fundamental right to vote.[1] Ironically, British suffragists in the early part of the twentieth century often targeted golf courses—the exclusive province of wealthy, privileged males—for their protests. Ron Rapoport in his book *The Immortal Bobby: Bobby Jones and the Golden Age of Golf* explains:

Politicians who played golf became a popular suffragette target—Lord Asquith, the prime minister, was assaulted by two women on the 17th green at Lossiemouth in northeastern Scotland—and the Royal and Ancient Guard took out insurance against damage to the course and recruited two hundred volunteers to serve as guards during the British Amateur Championship.[2]

In 1872 the U.S. Supreme Court ruled that a woman did not have a right to be a lawyer in the state of Illinois. In 1948, the Court upheld a Michigan law that disallowed women from serving as bartenders unless they were related to the bar owner.

ONE ATTORNEY'S FIGHT TO END COUNTRY CLUB GENDER DISCRIMINATION

Marsha V. Kazarosian is not an avid golfer but she may have done more for women golfers than nearly anyone in the United States. That is because she successfully litigated on behalf of nine women in Massachusetts who successfully sued a country club for nearly $2 million in damages. Kazarosian has tried cases since 1983, specializing in gender discrimination cases. She has handled many high-profile cases, including a male defendant in the Pamela Smart case. Smart was a woman who allegedly persuaded her underage lover to murder her husband.

Kazarosian does not back from a challenge, something she attributes to "being Armenian and stubborn." She would need those attributes in abundance when she represented Judith Borne, Sally Brochetti, Diana Cordner, Pamela Dean, Cindy Johnston, Lorna Kimball, Linda Letendre, Karen Richardson, and Maria Torrisi in an action of unlawful sex discrimination against the Haverhill Golf & Country Club. Kazarosian said that the women came to her because her secretary was a good friend of Sally Brochetti.

Originally eighteen women came to Kazarosian seeking legal redress for the discrimination they suffered at the country club. "Five dropped out, three were threatened by the club with IRS troubles and one died, leaving me with 9 plaintiffs," she said.[3]

In August 1995 the nine women filed a complaint with the Massachusetts Commission Against Discrimination alleging that the country club, a place of public accommodation under state law, discriminated against them because they were women. The plaintiffs alleged that the club discriminated on the basis of sex in terms of membership types. The "manipulation of membership types" occurred in stark terms as 318 of 325 primary memberships were filled by men, while 84 of the 90 limited memberships were filled by women.[4] The women-plaintiffs also contended that they had limited access to the golf course vis-à-vis the men. On Wednesdays, women limited players could not play from 10:00 a.m. to 2:00 p.m., and on Sundays women limited members could not play until after 11:30 a.m. The women also alleged instances of "unequal application of rules" in how the club disciplined women members as opposed to men members.[5]

"I never thought the case would go to trial," Kazarosian said. "I thought that reasonable minds would prevail. It was a tough case that lasted 8 and a half years. Many people would not have seen it through but I'm Armenian and very stubborn."[6]

The case did proceed to trial, where a jury awarded nearly $2 million in damages to Kazarosian's clients in October 1999. The country club appealed. In June 2003, the Massachusetts Court of Appeals affirmed the jury's verdict.

Apart from the direct evidence of discriminatory animus against women, there was ample evidence to take to the jury the question whether, concerning access to the golf links, the male officers of the Club rigged rules and applied rules in a manner that made women second class members, resulting in an uncomfortable and emotionally taxing environment at the Club for those women members who brought this action,

the appeals court wrote.[7]

The appeals court also refused to reduce the jury's sizable damage award against the country club. The court explained:

A jury, composed, as it is, of persons from varying walks of life and reflecting a variety of experience is a particularly suitable institution for assessing the emotional damage incident to being placed in a second class citizen status, made to feel inferior, socially ostracized, and demeaned in public. This was a form of discrimination freighted with economic side effects, and, therefore, the more susceptible to compensation in dollars.

Playing golf was not one of the unalienable rights of 1776, but it is naïve not to recognize the degree to which golf links and the country club are the locale for developing professional and business contacts. Golf and the country club lubricate the advance of careers. Deals are cut on the fairway and in the clubhouse.[8]

A further appeal to the Massachusetts Supreme Court was unsuccessful, as the state high exercised its discretionary jurisdiction and decided not to hear the appeal. Kazarosian said that with interest, attorneys, and damages, the entire award was in the neighborhood of $3.8 million.

"I think the decision empowered a lot of women to pursue what they think they're entitled to," Kazarosian said. "It was the first of its kind and it did give women a sense of power. The Borne case has done a lot with clubs to be receptive to changing their bylaws to end some discriminatory practices," Kazarosian says.

She says there are still plenty of private clubs that do discriminate and some can legally discriminate because their state law provides no protection against gender discrimination in places of public accommodation. "Discrimination against women at country clubs is still a huge problem," says Kazarosian. "Because of the way certain states have written their anti-discrimination statutes, some discriminatory action by private clubs is simply not actionable. And truly private clubs can discriminate based on their First Amendment right of freedom of association."

"In many ways, golf remains the last bastion of discrimination," she says. Discrimination will continue, she says, pointing out that she just recently settled another case of discrimination at a country club in May 2006.

However, she does continued progress in the future, as "more and more women make more money and have corporate positions that used to be reserved for men."[9]

TEED OFF AT UNFAIR TEE TIMES

Kazarosian's successful litigation on behalf of the nine women led to perhaps the definitive appellate decision prohibiting many forms of discrimination—at least in a state that has a broad public accommodations law. However, it was the first such lawsuit. In 1989, golfer Jan Bradshaw sued the Yorba Linda Country Club in California over its tee times. The country club gave men more hours on the course and also the better hours. Women were relegated to second-class citizens, according to Bradshaw and her famed attorney Gloria Allred.

"The situation at Yorba Linda golf club creates a gross inequality against women," Bradshaw told the *Los Angeles Times*.[10] Allred echoed her client's sentiments: "This lawsuit was her last recourse. This is a pioneering case, on the cutting edge of change for women in seeking to be first-class citizens on the golf course as well as in every other area of life."[11] Bradshaw's suit was settled out of court. It did lead to some changes in the club's policies on tee times.

After Bradshaw's suit, twenty-four single women filed a similar lawsuit in California against the Newport Beach Country Club. They claimed that they spent thousands more than single men for comparable memberships. The lead plaintiff in that case, Lynne Bennett, said: "It goes without saying that at many, if not most, golf clubs there is resistance to single women. To men, golf is a man's game and they don't want women on the course. They think women are in the way."[12]

Complaints of gender bias in golf are nothing new. In 1916, Anna Whitaker wrote a piece in the *Los Angeles Times* criticizing the Midwick Country Club for its exclusion of females. "To think that in this year of grace and woman's suffrage the Midwick Country Club should have the temerity to enact a female golfer exclusion act!"[13]

She criticized the directors of the Midwick club for issuing a "haughty ultimatum to the effect that no women may play on the course on Saturdays, and that if they play on Wednesdays they are to have no rights on the course and ungallant masculinity has the privilege of playing through!"[14]

AUGUSTA, HOOTIE, AND MARTHA

The most high-profile country club battle involving gender discrimination involved a very public feud between Martha Burk, chairwoman of the National Council of Women's Organizations, and William "Hootie" Johnson, chairman of the Augusta National Country Club in Augusta, Georgia—the club that hosts the most prestigious tournament in men's golf—The Masters.

Burk had read an article in the *USA TODAY* by sportswriter Christine Brennan that quoted Lloyd Ward, the then CEO of the United States Olympic Committee and one of the very few African-American members of

Augusta National. Ward had said: "I want to have influence on the inside. I want to talk to members of Augusta and say, quite frankly...you've got to have a broader membership, and that includes women."[15]

Burk, an ardent defender of women's rights who combats gender discrimination, wrote a letter to Johnson, stating in part:

Our member groups are very concerned that the nation's premier golf event, The Masters, is hosted by a club that discriminates against women by excluding them from membership. While we understand that there is no written policy barring women, Augusta National's Record speaks for itself. As you know, no woman has been invited to join since the club was formed in 1932.

We know that Augusta National and the sponsors of the Masters do not want to be viewed as entities that tolerate discrimination against any group, including women. We urge you to review your policies and practices in this regard, and open your membership to women now, so that this is not an issue when the tournament is staged next year.

Our leadership would be pleased to discuss this matter with you personally or by telephone. I will contact you in the next few weeks.[16]

Johnson and other club officials viewed Burk as an "attack activist," someone who was a very threat to the traditions of Augusta National, a historic exclusive and private club created in part by the great golfer Bobby Jones as a place where he and others could golf outside of the public view. Johnson responded with a public letter that he sent or e-mailed to more than eighty media outlets. His response read in part:

We take our membership very seriously. It is the very fabric of our club. Our members are people who enjoy each other's company and the game of golf. Our membership alone decides our membership—not any outside group with its own agenda....

There could be attempts at direct contact with board members of sponsoring corporations and inflammatory mailings to stockholders and investment institutions. We might see everything from picketing and boycotts to t-shirts and bumper stickers. On the Internet, there could be active chat rooms and e-mail messaging. These are all elements of such campaigns.

We certainly hope none of that happens. However, the message delivered to us was clearly coercive.

We will not be bullied, threatened or intimidated.

We do not intend to become a trophy in their display case.

There may well come a day when women will be invited to join our membership but that timetable will be ours and not at the point of a bayonet.[17]

Thus began the legendary battle of Augusta. Burk led a highly publicized protest of the club, placed pressure on corporate sponsors, and campaigned with other activist groups to force a chance in how Augusta National operated. Her public and, in some circles, controversial stance led her to receiving death threats. "I do watch my back when I come out my door at night," she said on CNN. "It is appalling to me that some people can get so worked up about this that I have to worry about my personal safety."[18]

Johnson and the club remained defiant until the end. Even when corporate television sponsors began to leave the Masters, the club abandoned corporate sponsors and hosted the tournament on its own. This meant that at least in 2003 the Masters was shown commercial free. Sponsors Coca Cola, General Motors, and Citibank left the Masters, though some sponsors—such as Exxon Mobil—did not. Augusta National still does not have a single female member.

The LPGA spoke out against the exclusionary practices of Augusta National. Ty Votaw, the then LPGA commissioner, emphasized that the LPGA tour represented women and the game of golf. "Augusta's exclusionary practices with respect to women speaks volumes," he said at the end of the women's 2002 season. "The message it sends is that women cannot be part of that face of golf. And that's wrong."[19] Votaw said the club's decision to treat gender differently than race is "perpetuating golf's exclusionary past and the perception that golf is elitist and exclusionary."[20] Some LPGA players spoke about the issue. Hall of Famer Juli Inkster said: "I can't believe we're still fighting this stuff—racism, gender equality. But that's life, I guess. It's not going to change overnight, but hopefully, in the coming years, it will change."[21]

Even though Burk was not able to convince Johnson to admit a female member, she shone a bright spotlight on a troubling issue. "Burk has certainly brought greater scrutiny to the propriety of all-male golf clubs in general and Augusta National in particular."[22]

TYPES OF DISCRIMINATION AGAINST WOMEN

For far too long, women have been excluded from the game of golf. Even today, membership to elite country clubs can be less than easy. Years ago it was not just private country clubs that served as bastions of bigotry; instead, it was city leaders. In 1968, city leaders in Omaha, Nebraska, refused to rescind a rule that limited women from playing on city golf courses on Saturday. "Women golfers are maddeningly slow and would drive the men crazy," said city council vice president Robert G. Cunningham.[23]

"It used to be overt and not as subtle," said famed California attorney Gloriia Allred. "Since women have started filing lawsuits, clubs have come up with new rules that gold memberships or primary memberships. Often that's just a code word for men."[24]

Professor Susan Cayleff explains that there used to hang in many clubhouses the slogan "G.O.L.F.," which stood for "Gentleman Only, Ladies Forbidden."[25] The mind-set can be difficult to change in a society that has been permeated with gender-based discrimination. Overcoming gender biases may be something that is never completely overcome. In 1972 U.S. male weight lifter

Russ Knipp responded after hearing that gymnast Olga Connelly would carry the American flag at the Munich Olympics: "The flag bearer ought to be a man, a strongman, a warrior. A woman's place is in the home."[26] A Connecticut trial court judge showed a similar mind-set when he said: "Athletic competition builds character in our boys. We do not need that kind of character in our girls."[27] Unfortunately, these types of comments are not unique and are not relegated to the 1970s. During its history, the LPGA tour even had to deal with threatened lawsuits from men who believed they were discriminated against because they were not allowed to join the LPGA tour.[28]

DISCRIMINATION OR FREEDOM OF ASSOCIATION

Club members often argue that maintaining an all-male club is not discrimination but protected freedom of association under the First

---

QUOTABLE: THE NEW YORK LAW AT ISSUE IN *NEW YORK STATE CLUB ASS'N v. CITY OF NEW YORK* (1988)

"It is hereby found and declared that the city of New York has a compelling interest in providing its citizens an environment where all persons, regardless of race, creed, color, national origin or sex, have a fair and equal opportunity to participate in the business and professional life of the city, and may be unfettered in availing themselves of employment opportunities. Although city, state and federal laws have been enacted to eliminate discrimination in employment, women and minority group members have not attained equal opportunity in business and the professions. One barrier to the advancement of women and minorities in the business and professional life of the city is the discriminatory practices of certain membership organizations where business deals are often made and personal contacts valuable for business purposes, employment and professional advancement are formed. While such organizations may avowedly be organized for social, cultural, civic or educational purposes, and while many perform valuable services to the community, the commercial nature of some of the activities occurring therein and the prejudicial impact of these activities on business, professional and employment opportunities of minorities and women cannot be ignored."

Source: Local Law No. 63 of 1984, § 1, App. 14–15.

Amendment. This is questionable given a series of cases decided by the U.S. Supreme Court involving all-male groups: *Roberts v. U.S. Jaycees* (1984),[29] *Board of Directors of Rotary v. Rotary Club of Duarte* (1987),[30] and *New York State Club Association v. City of New York* (1988).[31] Roberts involved the application of a Minnesota antidiscrimination law to an all-male Jaycees club that refused to allow women members. The Rotary Club case involved a similar situation of a Rotary Club that did not want to admit female members. Finally, the New York State Club Association involved a New York City law that sought to bring even private clubs within the umbrella of its antidiscrimination ordinance in part because some of those all-male clubs excluded women from important business opportunities and deal-making chances.

In these decisions the Court ruled that the club's private right to freedom of association was outweighed the state's compelling need to eradicate discrimination. The Court noted that the associational freedom was strongest for familial-type relations, not for organizations that truly were not private or selective. In *Roberts v. U.S. Jaycees* (1984), the Court explained:

By requiring the Jaycees to admit women as full voting members, the Minnesota Act works an infringement of the last type. There can be no clearer example of an intrusion into the internal structure or affairs of an association than a regulation that forces the group to accept members it does not desire. Such a regulation may impair the ability of the original members to express only those views that brought them together. Freedom of association therefore plainly presupposes a freedom not to associate.

The right to associate for expressive purposes is not, however, absolute. Infringements on that right may be justified by regulations adopted to serve compelling state interests, unrelated to the suppression of ideas, that cannot be achieved through means significantly less restrictive of associational freedoms.

We are persuaded that Minnesota's compelling interest in eradicating discrimination against its female citizens justifies the impact that application of the statute to the Jaycees may have on the male members' associational freedoms.

It remains an interesting legal question whether a private golf club is truly private enough to claim a constitutional free-association defense to a state public accommodations law.

The state will argue that it has a truly compelling, or very strong, interest in eradicating gender discrimination. A club could argue that such state intrusion infringes on its free-association rights. One legal commentator explained that

if a woman sued a private club for sex discrimination, the outcome may not be successful unless a state has an antidiscrimination law similar to the one in New York City. The crux of the test may depend on how much commercial activity takes place at the club and how often nonmembers are allowed into the club.[32]

The issue of whether there is a constitutional right of free-association on the part of these clubs is vital, because so many business opportunities are available from these clubs. Those who are locked out of the door never receive the opportunities as others do. Legal commentator Scott Rosner writes:

While many overt forms of discrimination have ended in the years since the Civil Rights Movement, problems persist in other areas of society. Private country clubs like Augusta National remain a hotbed of gender and racial discrimination, even as these clubs retain their importance to business and industry leaders. The expansion of the corporate boardroom to the golf courses, tennis courts, locker rooms, dining areas, and bars found at private country clubs provides members of these clubs with substantial business advantages and can further career advancement by allowing access to influential members of the business community, providing members with the ability to network and cultivate business relationships. Thus, access to country clubs is now more important than ever in the business world.[33]

LEGAL REDRESS

Obviously, there are major constitutional questions with respect to freedom of association as to whether the legal system can prohibit truly private discrimination. The Equal Protection Clause of the Fourteenth Amendment prohibits much intentional sexual and racial discrimination committed by the government. However, since the U.S. Supreme Court's 1883 ruling in *The Civil Rights Cases,* the Equal Protection Clause—that no state shall deny any person "equal protection of the law"—does not reach private conduct, it requires governmental, or state, action.

Congress passed the Civil Rights Act of 1964, part of which prohibits discrimination in places of public accommodation. However, the federal law since its inception has provided for an exception for private clubs. Thus, federal statutory law provides no vehicle for those seeking to break open the gates. There has been one member of Congress who has consistently sponsored federal legislation that would change the equation. That person is Representative Carolyn Maloney from New York.

On March 29, 2007, Maloney once again introduced the Ending Tax Breaks for Discrimination Act of 2007[34] and the Fair Play-Equal Access in Membership Resolution.[35] The tax bill would amend the Internal Revenue Code to prohibit tax deductions by individuals for dues paid to any private club that discriminates on the basis of sex, race, or color. The bill defines a private discriminatory club as "any club organized for business, pleasure, recreation, or other social purpose if such club restricts its membership or the use of its services or facilities on the basis of sex, race, or color."

"Men who belong to clubs like Augusta National reap financial benefits— either directly through tax deductions for business expenses or indirectly

THE FAIR PLAY—EQUAL ACCESS IN MEMBERSHIP RESOLUTION

CONCURRENT RESOLUTION

Expressing the sense of the Congress that neither the President, the Vice President, nor any Member of Congress, justice or judge of the United States, or political appointee in the executive branch of the Government should belong to a club that discriminates on the basis of sex or race.

Whereas Congress respects the right of private association;

Whereas the right of private association among friends, colleagues, and like-minded individuals is a deeply held American value when it is truly private, but is immorally invoked when it is used as a cover for discrimination;

Whereas the President, the Vice President, Members of Congress, justices and judges of the United States, and political appointees in the executive branch of the Government, by virtue of their public office, are obligated to adhere to a higher standard of conduct than what is minimally required by law, a standard of conduct that reflects the American value that discrimination is wrong; and

Whereas Members of Congress and other Government officials have recognized that membership in any club that discriminates is unacceptable for a public official, and have consequently resigned therefrom: Now, therefore, be it

Resolved by the House of Representatives (the Senate concurring),

Section 1. Short Title

This resolution may be cited as "the Fair Play—Equal Access in Membership Resolution."

Section 2. Sense of the Congress

It is the sense of the Congress that neither the President, the Vice President, nor any Member of Congress, justice or judge of the United States, or political appointee in the executive branch of the Government should belong to a club that discriminates on the basis of sex or race.

Source: H. Con. R. 107 (110th Congress).

through career opportunities and board appointments—that women can't get, just because they're women," said Maloney in a press release. "The American taxpayer shouldn't be subsidizing discrimination, period. These unfair writeoffs should be driven off the golf course and out of the tax code."[36]

Maloney's measures have never passed Congress and, seemingly, are not likely to in the near future. This means that legal redress must come through individual state statutes.

Some states have broad laws prohibiting discrimination by even private clubs. For example, Connecticut's law broadly prohibits any country club with a 9-hole golf course or more to discriminate based on race or gender. The law provides: "No golf country club may deny membership in such club to any person on account of race, religion, color, national origin, ancestry, sex, marital status or sexual orientation."[37] Another provision of the law provides: "All classes of membership in a golf country club shall be available without regard to race, religion, color, national origin, ancestry, sex, marital status or sexual orientation." New York, New Jersey, and Maryland have similar laws that reach even private clubs.

The solution then for women is to pressure state legislatures to enact broader public accommodations laws that will provide a sword against the discriminatory shield of certain private clubs. States can either broadly define places of public accommodation, use their licensing power to regulate liquor at private clubs, or deny property tax exemptions to country clubs that continue to discriminate.[38] But it may take the collective action of many women's groups and others to help wipe away the vestiges (or in some cases large collections) of discrimination.

Pam Swensen, chief executive officer of the Executive Women's Golf Association, explains a recent course of action that her group has launched:

In 2007, we introduced a "EWGA Female Friendly Designation" opportunity for golf facilities who are part of the EWGA Golf Club Network. To merit the designation, clubs must meet certain criteria rated on playability of the course and customer experience. Some of the factors include having at least two sets of tees rated for women, distance markers inside 100 yards, clean restrooms available at least every six holes and providing equal services to men and women. Women don't want to be treated differently—they just want to be taken seriously. This recognition program is a way for us to distinguish golf courses and management companies like Troon Golf (one of our strongest supporters) who understand the value of providing women friendly facilities. A satisfied woman customer means more business—it's the power of the purse again.[39]

—— CHAPTER 14 ——

THE FUTURE OF WOMEN'S GOLF

Sports, at their roots, are a reflection of society at large. There may also be some traces of bias in a society that still is male dominated. Consider that there has never been a female U.S. President, only two female members of the U.S. Supreme Court, and virtually no female coaches of men's professional sports. But society is improving. There are more than seventy female members of the U.S. House of Representatives and sixteen members in the U.S. Senate. There is a viable female Presidential candidate. In 2007, Kelly Tilghman serves as the PGA tour's first leading female announcer on the Golf Channel.[1] The sport has steadily made progress to the point where the LPGA tour provides millions and millions in purses to its top players.

"Women's golf has come a long way since the LPGA was founded in the early fifties," says Pam Swensen.

The original founding members of the LPGA would travel together from city to city—promote their tournaments, conduct clinics, mark their courses—they would do it all. And for practically no money even by 50's standards. Today, the depth and breadth of the LPGA is tremendous. It's big business and growing. The quality of the athletes is superior, purses have consistently been increasing, media interest has grown, web traffic is way up, the promotion of players is mainstream (i.e...Network TV appearances, media coverage in lifestyle magazines not just golf related magazines etc...). Competitive women's golf is a big business and growing.[2]

Some express concern that the women's game does not draw the same level of financial opportunity as the PGA men and the Seniors Tour. In 1989, Dottie Mochrie said: "I don't believe we'll ever come close to the men's game. It's not any one person's fault. It's nobody's fault. It's just the way it is." The men's tour simply has much more corporate money than the LPGA tour. Even the men's senior tour draws more corporate dollars than the top women's professionals. That remains a glaring disparity, as the women do not have a comparable seniors' tour. They may not have one in the near future. "I'm not sure if there will ever be a viable women's senior tour. I'm not sure corporate American wants to support watching older women play golf," says Janet Coles. "Additionally, there is a lot of money that is stretched thin already with the different tours."[3]

"I still think the women pro players need more recognition and respect," says Charles Mechem. "They deserve it. I still run into guys who say: 'Can they really play?'"[4] Of course, the answer is yes, as anyone who catches a glimpse of an Annika Sorenstam or Se Ri Pak can readily attest. Yet, recognition still needs to come to these deserving world-class athletes. "The women players are really such classy, talented human beings," says Mechem. "For years they played for less money with less attention and handled it with such great dignity."[5]

"On the professional side of the sport, the women who play on the LPGA Tour today are incredible and deserve to have the same earning potential as their male counterparts," says Swensen.

The LPGA is working on increasing the purses of their tournaments. However, it is incumbent upon women who are fans of the game to support the companies that support women's golf—and let them know they are making a difference. Women need to use their voice and their wallets to get the attention of businesses to know what a significant consumer base we are—only then will changes be made and recognition of equality be recognized and sought.

Swensen explains that the future of women's golf rests with the economic power of women. She elaborates:

Women are not a niche market anymore. So much has been written about marketing to women—and why companies should do this....If you are a business person and—it's all about the numbers—consider these facts:

Women and money—women account for more than 50 percent of all stock ownership in the US. By 2010, women will account for half of the private wealth in the country, or about $14 trillion.

Women and consumer and business spending—women control $7 trillion in consumer and business spending. They are responsible for or buy 94 percent of home furnishings, 91 percent of house purchases, 60 percent of cars and trucks and 50% of business travel.

Women and work—women-owned businesses employ more people in the US than the Fortune 500 companies employ. Today, women-owned businesses account for 33 percent of all firms in the country.

Women and education—in 2002, women earned 57% of the BA awarded in the US. In graduate programs, women now make up 49% of law school and 50% of medical school attendees.

Women and social norms—60% of adult women in America work outside of the home, up from about 30% in 1955. In 1955, 80% of Americans lived in a traditional nuclear family; in 2003 only 50% of Americans lived in that traditional social structure. Thirty percent of married women now out-earn their husbands; on top of that, there are now 46 million American women who are divorced, widowed or never married."[6]

In short, Swensen says that "women are transforming business and society. Women are changing—and they are changing everything with them: money, power, sex, family, technology and ultimately society."

Betsy Rawls said it best in 2005: "But golf is a wonderful game. There's something special about the world of golf. I don't know if the people are nicer or what, but it's a joy to be around it."[7]

The game of golf provides wonder to millions of women. In April 2007, 102-year-old woman Elise McLean hit a hole-in-one is Chico, California. Even more amazing, Sheila Drummond—a blind, 53-year-old woman—hit a hole-in-one at Mahoning Valley Country Club in Lehighton, PA.

More people would do well to bear in minds the words of Mr. Golf himself, Byron Nelson, who recognized the value of women's golf way back in 1946:

Don't ever belittle the influence of women in golf. They make up 60 percent of the spectators at our tournaments. And they'll be an even greater influence in the game because virtually every women's school and college is offering golf instruction as part of its athletic program.

Whenever my schedule allows it, I watch a women's championship event because I figure that I can always learn something watching them play. They haven't the power of the top men players, of course, but there isn't a male player today who couldn't learn something by watching the best women players in action.

For instance, you don't see good women players hurrying their back swings. They have marvelous short games. I particularly like to watch their finesse around the greens.[8]

APPENDICES

APPENDIX I: ALL-TIME LPGA MAJOR CHAMPIONSHIPS WON
(MINIMUM OF FIVE)

Name	Number
Patty Berg	15
Mickey Wright	13
Louise Suggs	11
Babe Zaharias	10
Annika Sorenstam	10
Betsy Rawls	8
Juli Inkster	7
Karrie Webb	6
Pat Bradley	6
Betsy King	6
Patty Sheehan	6
Kathy Whitworth	6
Amy Alcott	5
Se Ri Pak	5

For a far more detailed listing and statistics of LPGA major championship winners, see http://www.lpga.com/tournament_majors.aspx?mid=1&pid=38.

APPENDIX 2: PLAYERS WHOSE FIRST LPGA TOURNAMENT WIN WAS A MAJOR

Name	Tournament	Year
Betty Jameson	U.S. Women's Open	1947
Carol Mann	Western Open	1964
Laura Davies	U.S. Women's Open	1987
Liselotte Neumann	U.S. Women's Open	1988
Karrie Webb	British Open	1995
Se Ri Pak	LPGA Championship	1998
Birdie Kim	U.S. Women's Open	2005
Morgan Pressel	Kraft Nabisco	2007

APPENDIX 3: ALL-TIME LPGA TOURNAMENT WINNERS (AS OF MAY 6, 2007)

Raw Data Source: The Sports Network, "LPGA Tour—Women's Professional Golf; Statistics," 5/6/2007.

Author Number Crunching: Six women have won more than 50 LPGA tournaments; 26 women have won more than 20 LPGA tournaments; and 42 women have won more than 10 LPGA tournaments. By contrast, 95 women have won only one LPGA tournament.

Name	Number of Tournament Wins
Kathy Whitworth	88
Mickey Wright	82
Annika Sorenstam	69
Patty Berg	60
Louise Suggs	58
Betsy Rawls	55
Nancy Lopez	48
JoAnne Carner	42
Sandra Haynie	42
Babe Zaharias	41
Carol Mann	40
Patty Sheehan	35
Karrie Webb	35
Betsy King	34
Beth Daniel	33
Pat Bradley	31
Juli Inkster	31
Amy Alcott	29
Jane Blalock	29
Judy Rankin	26
Marlene Hagge	25
Donna Caponi	24

Se Ri Pak	24
Marilyn Smith	22
Sandra Palmer	21
Laura Davies	20
Meg Mallon	18
Hollis Stacy	18
Ayako Okamoto	17
Dottie Pepper	17
Jan Stephenson	16
Sally Little	15
Lorena Ochoa	15
Rosie Jones	13
Liselotte Neumann	13
Susie Berning	11
Clifford Ann Creed	11
Shirley Englehorn	11
Jane Geddes	11
Ruth Jessen	11
Mary Lena Faulk	10
Betty Jameson	10
Chris Johnson	9
Cristie Kerr	9
Kelly Robbins	9
Colleen Walker	9
Mi Hyun Kim	9
Alice Miller	8
Mary Mills	8
Sandra Post	8
Rachel Teske	8
Danielle Ammaccapane	7
Debbie Austin	7
Tammie Green	7
Michelle McGann	7
Sandra Spuzich	7
Sherri Steinhauer	7
Donna Andrews	6
Kathy Cornelius	6
Hee-Won Han	6
Grace Park	6
Jo Ann Prentice	6
Val Skinner	6
Helen Alfredsson	5
Brandie Burton	5
Pat Hurst	5
Barb Mucha	5
Cindy Rarick	5
Deb Richard	5
Silvia Bertolaccini	4
Murle Breer	4
Betty Burfeindt	4

C. J. Callison Whitted	4
Dorothy Delasin	4
Judy Dickinson	4
Sophie Gustafson	4
Penny Hammel	4
Lorie Kane	4
Hiromi Kobayashi	4
Alison Nicholas	4
Kathy Postlewait	4
Patti Rizzo	4
Sue Roberts	4
Wendy Ward	4
Mary Beth Zimmerman	4
Kathy Ahern	3
Dawn Coe-Jones	3
Paula Creamer	3
Betsy Cullen	3
Wendy Doolan	3
Dale Eggeling	3
Cathy Gerring	3
Shelley Hamlin	3
Pam Higgins	3
Trish Johnson	3
Judy Kimball Simon	3
Emilee Klein	3
Candie Kung	3
Debbie Massey	3
Lauri Merten	3
Terry-Jo Myers	3
Martha Nause	3
Nancy Scranton	3
Muffin Spencer-Devlin	3
Sherri Turner	3
Lisa Walters	3
Jo Ann Washam	3
Donna White	3
Maggie Will	3
Jody Anschutz	2
Jerilyn Britz	2
Janet Coles	2
Elaine Crosby	2
Heather Daly-Donofrio	2
Laura Diaz	2
Dana Dormann	2
Gloria Ehret	2
Jan Ferraris	2
Akiko Fukushima	2
Gail Graham	2
Kathy Guadagnino	2
Cindy Hill	2

Maria Hjorth	2
Jeong Jang	2
Christina Kim	2
Carin Koch	2
Bonnie Lauer	2
Meena Lee	2
Brittany Lincicome	2
Catriona Matthew	2
P. Meunier-Lebouc	2
Sharon Miller	2
Kris Monaghan	2
Janice Moodie	2
Anne-Marie Palli	2
Gloria Park	2
Stacy Prammanasudh	2
Penny Pulz	2
Michele Redman	2
Laurie Rinker-Graham	2
Jenny Rosales	2
Karen Stupples	2
Lynn Adams	1
Shi Hyun Ahn	1
Kristi Albers	1
Janet Anderson	1
M. Astrologes Combs	1
Marisa Baena	1
Pam Barnett	1
Sharon Barrett	1
Tina Barrett	1
Barbara Barrow	1
Missie Berteotti	1
Jocelyne Bourassa	1
Nanci Bowen	1
Heather Bowie	1
Bonnie Bryant	1
Barb Bunkowsky	1
Silvia Cavalleri	1
Mei-Chi Cheng	1
Jane Crafter	1
Mary Lou Crocker	1
Florence Descampe	1
Helen Dobson	1
Moira Dunn	1
Michelle Estill	1
Vicki Fergon	1
Cindy Figg-Currier	1
Marta Figueras-Dotti	1
Allison Finney	1
Tina Fischer	1
Meaghan Francella	1

Amy Fruhwirth	1
Shirley Furlong	1
J. Gallagher-Smith	1
Lori Garbacz	1
Dorothy Germain	1
Kate Golden	1
Julieta Granada	1
Patty Hayes	1
Carolyn Hill	1
Mayumi Hirase	1
Kathy Hite-James	1
Jin Joo Hong	1
Robin Hood	1
Lauren Howe	1
Becky Iverson	1
Cathy Johnston-Forbes	1
Patty Jordan	1
Jimin Kang	1
Soo-Yun Kang	1
Laurel Kean	1
Tracy Kerdyk	1
Lisa Kiggens	1
Birdie Kim	1
Joo Mi Kim	1
Ok Hee Ku	1
Kelli Kuehne	1
Jee Young Lee	1
Seon Hwa Lee	1
Jenny Lidback	1
Hilary Lunke	1
Mardi Lunn	1
Cindy Mackey	1
Kathryn Marshall	1
Margie Masters	1
Susie McAllister	1
Missie McGeorge	1
Caroline McMillan	1
Melissa McNamara	1
Pat Meyers	1
Cathy Morse	1
Catrin Nilsmark	1
Becky Pearson	1
Nicole Perrot	1
Julie Piers	1
Joan Pitcock	1
Mary Bea Porter-King	1
Morgan Pressel	1
Sally Quinlan	1
Cathy Reynolds	1
Lenore Rittenhouse	1

Barbara Romack	1
Kim Saiki	1
Cindy Schreyer	1
Pearl Sinn	1
Beth Solomon	1
Charlotta Sorenstam	1
Shirley G. Spork	1
Angela Stanford	1
Tina Tombs	1
Gail Toushin	1
Kris Tschetter	1
Barb Whitehead	1
Peggy Wilson	1
Jennifer Wyatt	1
Sung Ah Yim	1

APPENDIX 4: PLAYER OF THE YEAR AWARDS

Name	Year
Kathy Whitworth	1966
Kathy Whitworth	1967
Kathy Whitworth	1968
Kathy Whitworth	1969
Sandra Haynie	1970
Kathy Whitworth	1971
Kathy Whitworth	1972
Kathy Whitworth	1973
JoAnne Carner	1974
Sandra Palmer	1975
Judy Rankin	1976
Judy Rankin	1977
Nancy Lopez	1978
Nancy Lopez	1979
Beth Daniel	1980
JoAnne Carner	1981
JoAnne Carner	1982
Patty Sheehan	1983
Betsy King	1984
Nancy Lopez	1985
Pat Bradley	1986
Ayako Okamoto	1987
Nancy Lopez	1988
Betsy King	1989
Beth Daniel	1990
Pat Bradley	1991
Dottie Pepper	1992
Betsy King	1993
Beth Daniel	1994
Annika Sorenstam	1995

Laurie Davies	1996
Annika Sorenstam	1997
Annika Sorenstam	1998
Karrie Webb	1999
Karrie Webb	2000
Annika Sorenstam	2001
Annika Sorenstam	2002
Annika Sorenstam	2003
Annika Sorenstam	2004
Annika Sorenstam	2005
Lorena Ochoa	2006

Source: LPGA at http://www.lpga.com/content_1.aspx?mid=2&pid=2500.

APPENDIX 5: MULTIPLE PLAYER OF THE YEAR WINNERS (ROLEX)

Name	Number
Kathy Whitworth	7
Annika Sorenstam	7
Nancy Lopez	4
JoAnne Carner	3
Betsy King	3
Beth Daniel	3
Karrie Webb	2
Judy Rankin	2
Pat Bradley	2

APPENDIX 6: MOST LPGA HOLES-IN-ONE

Name	Number
Kathy Whitworth	11
Mickey Wright	8
Meg Mallon	8
Jan Stephenson	8
Betsy King	7
Pat Bradley	6
Marlene Bauer Hagge	6
Marilyn Smith	5
Beth Daniel	5
Ayako Okamoto	5
Hollis Stacy	4
Carol Mann	4
Dottie Pepper	4
Jane Blalock	4
Annika Sorenstam	3
JoAnne Carner	3
Nancy Lopez	3
Patty Sheehan	3

Notes

Chapter 1. Golf's Origins

1. F. W. Crane, "What Women Can Do in Golf," *New York Times,* July 4, 1897, 1WM4.

2. "The Golf Craze," *New York Times,* September 13, 1897, 4.

3. F. Johnston Roberts, "Woman's Prowess on Golf Links," *New York Times,* October 3, 1897, SM4.

4. Quoted in "Golf Is the Coming Game," *Chicago Tribune,* August 7, 1892, 35.

5. "Golf Is the Coming Game," *Chicago Tribune,* August 7, 1892, 35.

6. Dale Concannon, *Golf: The Early Days* (Vancouver, Canada: Cavendish Books, 1995), 10.

7. Ibid., 10–12.

8. Robert Sommers, *Golf Anecdotes: From the Links of Scotland to Tiger Woods* (New York: Oxford University Press, 1995), 11.

9. Concannon, *Golf: The Early Days,* 10.

10. Ibid., 22.

11. Ibid., 23.

12. John Guy, *The True Life of Mary Stuart: Queen of Scots* (New York: Houghton Mifflin Co., 2004), 146.

13. Antonia Fraser, *Mary Queen of Scots* (New York: Random House, 1969), 179.

14. Alison Weir, *Mary Queen of Scots and the Murder of Lord Darnley* (New York: Random House, 2003), 342.

15. Elinor Nickerson, *Golf: A Women's History* (Jefferson, NC: McFarland & Company, Inc., 1987), 11.

16. "Women Who Delight in Athletics," *Chicago Daily Tribune,* December 24, 1893, 6.

17. Rhonda Glenn, *The Illustrated History of Women's Golf* (Texas: Taylor Trade Publishing, 1991), 7.

18. Nickerson, *Golf: A Women's History,* 11.

19. Glenn, *The Illustrated History of Women's Golf,* 9.

20. "For and About Women," *Atlanta Constitution,* July 29, 1893, 9.

21. Ibid., 15.

22. Ibid., 16.

23. Ibid., 17.

24. Ibid., 18.

25. Personal communication, Gillian Kirkwood, May 2007.

26. Ibid.

27. "Fall of the Game of Lawn Tennis," *Chicago Daily Tribune,* August 8, 1896, 13.

28. "Girls Taking to Golf," *Washington Post,* July 27, 1890, 15.

29. "Golf Is Growing in New York," *New York Times,* October 4, 1891, 20.

30. Ibid.

31. "Golf Is the Coming Game," *Chicago Tribune,* August 7, 1892, 35.

32. "Authors and Reader," *Los Angeles Times,* April 2, 1893, 18.

33. "College Girls' Golf," *Chicago Daily Tribune,* May 20, 1893, 16.

34. "Society's Latest Pastime," *New York Times,* June 10, 1894, 16.

35. "Golf Now Their Amusement," *New York Times,* July 4, 1894, 3.

36. Diana Crossways, "By Women—For Women," *Los Angeles Times,* October 13, 1895, 26.

37. "Women Who Play Good Golf: Opening of the Ladies' Tournament at Morristown," *New York Times,* October 18, 1894, 3.

38. "Played by Fair Golfers: Interesting Contest on the Morris-County Club's Links," *New York Times,* October 20, 1894, 7.

39. "Golf Matches at Shinnecock," *New York Times,* October 28, 1894, 14.

40. "Newport Turns to Golf: Women Who Are Expert Players," *New York Times,* August 18, 1895, 13.

41. "Mrs. Duncan Won," *New York Times,* September 6, 1895, 10.

42. "Devoted to Sport: American Women Are Growing More and More Athletic," *Chicago Daily Tribune,* August 25, 1894, 16.

43. "Athletic Grandmammas," *Los Angeles Times,* February 27, 1895, 6.

44. "Women at the Golf Links," *New York Times,* October 7, 1896, 3.

45. Ibid.

46. F.W. Crane, "The Golf Season of 1896," *New York Times,* December 6, 1896, SM4.

CHAPTER 2. EARLY GREATS OF THE GAME

1. Personal communication, Rhonda Glenn, April 2007.

2. "Whigham Takes on Golf," *New York Times,* December 5, 1897, 16.

3. Ibid.

4. "Golf a Popular Fad," *Washington Post,* November 10, 1893, 8.

5. Ibid.

6. "Women Players on the Golf Links," *Chicago Daily Tribune,* April 25, 1897, 4.

7. "American Golfers Lose," *New York Times,* May 26, 1905, 7.

8. Personal communication, Glenn, April 2007.

9. "Famous Women Golfers," *New York Times,* April 19, 1908, S3.

10. "Women at the Golf Links," *New York Times,* October 8, 1896, 8.

11. Ibid., October 27, 1896, 3.

12. F.W. Crane, "The Golf Season of 1896," *New York Times,* December 6, 1896, SM4.

13. "Miss Hoyt and Sands Win," *New York Times,* November 6, 1897, 4.

14. "Miss Hoyt Golf Champion," *New York Times,* December 16, 1898, 4.

15. Associated Press, "Feminine Golf Classic Fixed," *Los Angeles Times,* May 8, 1931, A11.

16. Associated Press, "Golf Trophy Offered by the Curtis Sisters For Women's Matches Is Declined by British," *New York Times,* April 27, 1932, 21.

17. Associated Press, "English Accept Bid to Women's Golf Team; Will Mark First Official Invasion of U.S.," *New York Times,* February 8, 1934, 25.

18. Associated Press, "Miss Campbell's Cup," *Washington Post,* October 10, 1909, 53.

19. Associated Press, "Mary Browne is Defeated," *Los Angeles Times,* September 7, 1924, 11.

20. Joyce Wethered, *Golfing Memories and Methods* (London, England: Hutchinson & Co., 1934), 40.

21. Bobby Jones, "'Bobby' Says Alexa Stirling Has Good Chance to Win," *Atlanta Constitution,* May 30, 1921, 1.

22. Mark Frost, *The Grand Slam* (New York: Good Comma Ink, 2004), 22–23.

23. Ibid.

24. Chick Evans, "Tee Fairway and Green," *Los Angeles Times,* December 30, 1923, 111.

25. Stephanie Mansfield, "After 83 Years She Still Has That Swing," *Washington Post,* October 5, 1982, A1.

26. Edith Cummings Munson Golf Award, at http://www.ngca.com/i4a/pages/index.cfm?pageid=3306.

27. Kenan Helse, "Virginia Van Wie; Won 3 Amateur Golf Titles," *Chicago Tribune,* February 22, 1997, 19N.

28. Quoted in Melanie Credle, "Swing Time," *Herald-Sun* (Durham, NC), April 13, 1997, E1.

29. Rhonda Glenn, "Maureen Orcutt, Winner of 2 USGA Events, Dies at 99," USGA.com, January 10, 2007, http://www.usga.org/news/2007/january/orcutt_obit.html.

30. Paul R. Michelson, "Helen Hicks Cops Crown," *Los Angeles Times,* September 13, 1929, A11.

31. "Helen Hicks Wins, 2 and 1; Queen of U.S. Golf," *Chicago Daily Tribune,* September 27, 1931, A1.

32. Ibid.

33. Helen Hicks, "Helen Hicks Reviews Amazing Upset of Americans in First-Round Golf Matches," *Los Angeles Times,* May 31, 1932, A18.

34. Bob Cavagnaro, "Helen Hicks Retires from Amateur Golf," *Los Angeles Times,* June 20, 1934, A9.

35. Ibid.

36. Associated Press, "Being Pro Is Great, Says Helen Hicks," *Washington Post,* February 14, 1935, 14.

37. Charles Bartlett, "Helen Hicks Wins Western Open Golf Title," *Chicago Daily Tribune,* June 20, 1937, B1.

38. "Women's P.G.A. Plan Proposed by Helen Hicks," *Chicago Daily Tribune,* January 21, 1944, 22.

39. "Who Won," *Time Magazine,* September 13, 1937, http://www.time.com/time/magazine/article/0,9171,770859,00.html?promoid=googlep.

40. "'Damned Nuisance' Girl Who Went on to Become a Top Woman Golfer," *Derby Evening Telegraph,* November 13, 2006, 26.

41. Ibid.

42. Quoted in Patricia Davies, "The First Lady of Curtis Cup Is Back," *Times* (London), June 8, 1988.

43. "'Damned Nuisance' Girl Who Went on to Become a Top Woman Golfer," *Derby Evening Telegraph,* November 13, 2006, 26.

44. Joyce Wethered, *Golfing Memories and Methods* (London, England: Hutchinson & Co., 1934), 67.

45. Byron Nelson, "Mr. Golf Tees Off," *Chicago Daily Tribune,* April 2, 1946, 24.

CHAPTER 3. JOYCE WETHERED—THE GREATEST FEMALE GOLFER EVER

1. Basil Ashton Tinkler, *Joyce Wethered: The Great Lady of Golf* (Stroud, Glouchester: Tempus Publishing Limited 2004), 47.

2. Dave Anderson, "Sarazen's Century of Perspective," *New York Times,* May 16, 1999, SP4.

3. Quoted in Tinkler, *Joyce Wethered: The Great Lady of Golf,* 47.

4. Ibid., 48.

5. Bobby Jones, "The Greatest of Golfers: A Tribute to the Rare Skill of Miss Joyce Wethered," *American Golfer,* 1930.

6. Joyce Wethered, *Golfing Memories and Methods* (London, England: Hutchinson & Co., 1934), 36.

7. Alexa W. Stirling, "Miss Alexa Stirling Pays High Compliments to Her Opponents in British Championship," *Atlanta Constitution,* July 10, 1921, A2.

8. Ibid.

9. Tinkler, *Joyce Wethered: The Great Lady of Golf,* 39.

10. Associated Press, "Miss Cecil Leitch Loses Golf Crown," *New York Times,* May 20, 1922, 18.

11. Tinkler, *Joyce Wethered: The Great Lady of Golf,* 65.

12. Associated Press, "100 Women Start British Golf Today," *New York Times,* May 18, 1925, 11.

13. Quoted in Don Skeene, "Joyce Wethered Eliminates Glenna Collett in Troon Tournament," *Los Angeles Times,* May 21, 1925, B1.

14. Tinkler, *Joyce Wethered: The Great Lady of Golf,* 74.

15. Ibid.

16. Quoted in Associated Press, "Miss Wethered Quits Major Golf Play, 'Simply Because I Choose To,' She Says," *New York Times,* June 25, 1925, 17.

17. Associated Press, "Oblivious to Roar of Train, Miss Wethered Sinks Putt," *New York Times,* February 10, 1926, 18.

18. Wethered, *Golfing Memories and Methods,* 65.

19. Associated Press, "Marion Turpie Defeated in Upset," *Washington Post,* May 14, 1929, 15.

20. Tinkler, *Joyce Wethered: The Great Lady of Golf,* 123.

21. Ibid., 128.

22. Henry C. Crouch, "British Golf Title to Miss Wethered," *New York Times,* May 18, 1929, 19.

23. Wethered, *Golfing Memories and Methods,* 75.

24. Ibid., 105.

25. Associated Press, "Miss Wethered Beats Tolley, 2 and 1, Aided by Handicap," *New York Times,* June 6, 1930, 31.

26. See http://www.curtiscup.org/2004/history/index.html.

27. Helen Hicks, "Superior U.S. Play Decided Foursomes," *New York Times,* May 22, 1932, S6.

28. Ibid.

29. Quoted in W.F. Leysmith, "U.S. Women Golfers Beat British Team," *New York Times,* May 22, 1932, S1.

30. Associated Press, "Miss Wethered Gets a Job," *New York Times,* February 7, 1933, 25.

31. John Steele, "Is Wethered an Amateur, or _ ? British Wonder," *Chicago Daily Tribune,* February 8, 1933, 15.

32. Harry L. Percy, "Enid Wilson's Entry Refused for British Women's Tourney," *Los Angeles Times,* April 27, 1934, A9.

33. Arthur J. Daley, "Miss Wethered Here to Embark on Career as a Pro Golf Player," *New York Times,* May 28, 1935, 34.

34. Charles Barlett, "Joyce Wethered and Smith Win Golf Exhibition," *Chicago Daily Tribune,* July 8, 1935, 18.

35. Nelson, "Mr. Golf Tees Off."

36. Quoted in Associated Press, "Patty Berg Is Standout in England," *Washington Post,* April 28, 1936, 16.

37. Associated Press, "Patty Berg Wins Twice," *Los Angeles Times,* April 28, 1936, A13.

38. Frank Litsky, "Joyce Wethered, 96, Top Golfer of the 20s," *New York Times,* November 25, 1997, D24.

CHAPTER 4. THE BABE AND THE BERG...AND LOUISE SUGGS

1. Fred Corcoran with Bud Harvey, *Unplayable Lies: The Story of Sport's Most Successful Impressario* (New York: Meredith Press, 1965), 166.

2. James F. Fowler, "Century's Top Woman Star? Babe Didrikson—Who Else?" *Washington Post,* February 16, 1950, 17.

3. Susan E. Cayleff, *Babe Didrikson: The Greatest All-Sport Athlete of All Time* (Berkeley, CA: Conari Press, 1995), 11.

4. Ibid., 18.

5. Ibid., 51.

6. Associated Press, "I.W.A.C. Wins Team Title in National Meet," *Chicago Daily Tribune,* July 26, 1931, A2.

7. United Press, "Crown Lost by Stella Walsh: 'Babe' Didrickson Sets World Marks in A.A.U. Meet," *Washington Post,* July 26, 1931, M17.

8. Muriel Babcock, "All Records to Go Boom," *Los Angeles Times,* July 23, 1932, 7.

9. Grantland Rice, "The Sportlight," *Los Angeles Times,* July 29, 1932, A15.

10. Braven Dyer, "Five Marks Broken in Olympics: Babe Didrickson Cracks World Javelin Record," August 1, 1932, *Los Angeles Times,* 9.

11. Grantland Rice, "Sudden Rule Defeats Babe," *Los Angeles Times,* August 8, 1932, 13.

12. Ibid.

13. Grantland Rice, "Babe Breaks Records Easier than Dishes," *Los Angeles Times,* August 4, 1932, 11.

14. Associated Press, "Miss Didrickson to Play in U.S. Title Golf; Dallas Welcomes Olympic Star with Parade," *New York Times,* August 12, 1932, 21.

15. Cayleff, *Babe Didrikson,* 89.

16. Ibid., 93.

17. Ibid., 98.

18. Ibid., 101.

19. "Tee-Hee! The Golfer was Babe," *Washington Post,* May 5, 1935, B2.

20. Cayleff, *Babe Didrikson,* 119.

21. Ibid., 123.

22. Ibid., 125.

23. Bus Ham, "The Gals Tee Off on the Babe," *Washington Post,* January 24, 1954, C1.

24. Steve Trivett, "Bigger than Life, Babe's Legacy Lives on with LPGA," *Denver Post,* June 20, 2005, 27S.

25. Associated Press, "Mrs. Zaharias Is First American to Win Women's British Golf Title," *New York Times,* June 13, 1947, 1.

26. Ibid.

27. Glenn, *The Illustrated History of Women's Golf,* 139.

28. Ibid., 140.

29. Cayleff, *Babe Didrikson,* 133.

30. Associated Press, "Babe Zaharias Wins Top Honor," *Los Angeles Times,* February 16, 1950, C1.

31. Corcoran, *Unplayable Lies,* 182.

32. Associated Press, "Babe Zaharias' Sports Career Ended! Hit by Malignant Malady," *Chicago Daily Tribune,* April 10, 1953, B1.

33. Bill Rives, "Babe Zaharias' Toughest Battle," *Sport* (September 1953), in *The Best of Sport: Classic Writing From the Golden Era of Sports* (Toronto: Sportclassic Books, 2003), 27–35, 30.

34. Ibid.

35. "Comeback Honor Goes to the Babe," *Chicago Daily Tribune,* January 16, 1954, A4.

36. Jim Murray, "The Other Babe," *Los Angeles Times,* December 5, 1975, C1.

37. "Amazing 41-Year-Old Won Battle with Cancer," *Washington Post,* December 22, 1954, 28.

38. Patty Berg, "Babe Graced Sports with Her Skill and Courage," *New York Times,* July 15, 1984, 189.

39. Cayleff, *Babe Didrikson,* 158.

40. Ibid., 159.

41. John Gonella, "This Week We Play as Tribute to Babe," *Washington Post,* June 21, 1953, C3.

42. Jim Murray, "The Other Babe," *Los Angeles Times,* December 5, 1975, C1.

43. Elinor Nickerson, *Golf: A Women's History* (Jefferson, NC: McFarland & Company, Inc., 1987), 46.

44. See "Top N. American Athletes of the Century," http://espn.go.com/sports century/athletes.html.

45. Personal communication, Susan Cayleff, April 2007.

46. Quoted in "Patricia Jane Berg: Feb 13, 1998—Sept. 10, 2006," *News-Press* (Fort Myers, FL), 10A.

47. Ibid.

48. Nelson, "Mr. Golf Tees Off."

49. Arthur Daley, "She Now Tells It to the Marines," *New York Times,* January 10, 1944, 21.

50. Judy L. Hasday, *Extraordinary Women Athletes* (New York: Children's Press, 2000), 41.

51. Liz Kahn, *The Lpga: The Unauthorized Version: The History of the Ladies Professional Golf Association* (Group Fore Productions, 1996), 13.

52. Ibid.

53. Ibid.

54. "Crosby and Hope Bow to Feminine Golfers," *Los Angeles Times,* January 20, 1941, 15.

55. Associated Press, "Patty Berg Hurt in Automobile Crash in Texas," *Washington Post,* December 9, 1941, 26.

56. Ibid.

57. Associated Press, "Links Career Not in Jeopardy," *New York Times,* December 11, 1941, 41.

58. "Pulling for a Comeback," *New York Times,* January 7, 1943, 27.

59. Charles Bartlett, "Patty Berg Wins Western Open Title, 1 Up," *Chicago Daily Tribune,* July 3, 1943, 13.

60. Arthur Daley, "She Now Tells It to the Marines," *New York Times,* January 10, 1944, 21.

61. "Patty Berg No. 1 in Athletic Poll," *New York Times,* December 21, 1943, 33.

62. Associated Press, "Miss Berg Doffs Uniform of Marine for Golf Bags," *New York Times,* September 16, 1945, S6.

63. "Patty Berg Stages Great Rally to Beat Mrs. Zaharias in Western Open Golf," *New York Times,* June 27, 1948, S5.

64. "Patty Berg Beats Mrs. Zacharias in Woman Athlete of 1955 Poll," *New York Times,* January 6, 1956, 26.

65. Bus Ham, "The Gals Tee Off on Babe," *Washington Post,* January 24, 1954, C1.

66. Kahn, *The Lpga,* 11.

67. Personal communication, April 2007.

68. Quoted in Rhonda Glenn, "Berg, LPGA Founder, Dies at 88," USGA.com, September 10, 2006, http://www.usga.org/news/2006/september/berg.html.

69. Associated Press, "Miss Suggs Defeats Mrs. Zaharias in Western Open Semi-Final, 1 Up," *New York Times,* June 29, 1946, 15.

70. Charles Bartlett, "Louise Suggs Wins Western Open Golf Title," *Chicago Daily Tribune,* June 30, 1946, A1.

71. Ibid.

72. Associated Press, "Louise Suggs Rising Star Among Golfers," *Washington Post,* March 23, 1942, 17.

73. Quoted in Associated Press, "Louise Suggs Wins 7th Major Golf Title of 46 —the Western Open," *Chicago Daily Tribune,* A1.

74. Charles Curtis, "Gal Golfers Beat Guys," *Los Angeles Times,* September 23, 1948, C2.

75. West McLean, "Suggs Wins Women's Open Title," *Washington Post,* September 26, 1949, 11.

76. Associated Press, "Suggs Takes Women's Open on Record 2084," *Chicago Daily Tribune,* June 30, 1952, C3.

77. Lincoln A. Werden, "Miss Suggs Captures National Open Golf by 7 Strokes with Record 284 Score," *New York Times,* June 30, 1952, 24.

78. Lincoln A. Werden, "Louise Suggs Takes Weathervane Cross-Country Golf by 11-Stroke Margin," *New York Times,* June 1, 1953, 28.

79. Oscar Fraley, "Suggs Beats Male Pros in Par-3 Golf," *Washington Post,* February 16, 1961, D1; Associated Press, "Louise Suggs Proves Gal Golfers Can Beat Men; Snead Victim," *Los Angeles Times,* February 16, 1961, C1.

CHAPTER 5. FORMING THE LPGA AND OTHER GREATS OF THAT ERA

1. World Golf Hall of Fame Profile: Marlene Bauer Hagge, http://www.wgv.com/hof/member.php?member=1056.

2. Elinor Nickerson, *Golf: A Women's History* (Jefferson, NC: McFarland & Company, Inc., 1987), 51.

3. Glenn, *The Illustrated History of Women's Golf,* 155.

4. Corcoran, *Unplayable Lies,* 166.

5. Glenn, *The Illustrated History of Women's Golf,* 159.

6. Corcoran, *Unplayable Lies,* 167.

7. Amy Engeler, "For Women Golfers, Life in the Rough," *New York Times,* October 1, 1989, SM42.

8. Corcoran, *Unplayable Lies,* 167.

9. Ibid., 171.

10. Personal communication, Susan Cayleff, April 2007.

11. "Corcoran Takes the Gals," *Washington Post,* March 21, 1952, B4.

12. Quoted in Tom Tomashek, "The Founders of the LPGA Tour Fondly Look Back..." *News Journal* (Wilington, DE), June 18, 2000, 16L.

13. Ibid.

14. Corcoran, *Unplayable Lies*, 175.

15. Ibid., 178.

16. Quoted in Kelly Landy, "Game for the Ages; LPGA's Jameson Honored with Event That Also Benefits Palm Beach Juniors," *Sun-Sentinel* (Fort Lauderdale, FL), February 5, 2006, 2B.

17. Quoted in Bob Baptist, "2005 Honoree Betsy Rawls; A Real Problem-Solver," *Columbus Dispatch* (OH), May 31, 2005, 4C.

18. World Golf Hall of Fame Profile: Marlene Bauer Hagge, http://www.wgv.com/hof/member.php?member=1056.

19. World Golf Hall of Fame Profile: Marilyn Smith, http://www.wgv.com/hof/member.php?member=1131.

CHAPTER 6. THE TWO GREATEST WINNERS: MICKEY WRIGHT AND
KATHY WHITWORTH

1. Bill Fields, "The Wright Stuff," *Golf World,* November 24, 2000, http://www.golfdigest.com/newsandtour/index.ssf?/features/the_wrig-1yatttfc.html.

2. Quoted in "Mickey Wright Has Surgery for Breast Cancer," *USA TODAY,* October 27, 2006, http://www.usatoday.com/sports/golf/lpga/2006-10-27-wright-cancer_x.htm.

3. Associated Press, "Mickey Wright Wants to Become Best Golfer," *Washington Post,* June 10, 1956, C2.

4. Bill Fields, "The Wright Stuff," *Golf World,* November 24, 2000, http://www.golfdigest.com/newsandtour/index.ssf?/features/the_wrig-1yatttfc.html.

5. Associated Press, "Zaharias Wins Women's Open—291," *Los Angeles Times,* July 4, 1954, B10.

6. Associated Press, "Wright is Top Woman in Sports," *Washington Post,* January 5, 1964, C4.

7. Kathy Whitworth, "My Shot: Kathy Whitworth," *Golf Digest,* July 2005, http://www.golfdigest.com/features/index.ssf?/features/gd200507whitworth.html.

8. Lisa D. Mackey, "Three LPGA Aces," *Golf Digest,* December 2000, http://www.golfdigest.com/features/index.ssf?/features/three_lp_pa6z1fc.html.

9. Kathy Whitworth interviewed by Guy Yocum, "My Shot: Kathy Whitworth," GolfDigest.com, July 2005, http://www.golfdigest.com/features/index.ssf?/features/gd200507whitworth.html.

10. Associated Press, "Kathy Whitworth Top Girl Athlete of 1965," *Los Angeles Times,* January 14, 1966, B7.

11. Associated Press, "Kathy Whitworth Again Voted Top Female Athlete of Year," *Washington Post,* January 17, 1967, C2.

12. Kent Hannon, "Kathy Whitworth: Back on Her Game," *New York Times,* May 17, 1982, C8.

13. United Press International, "Miss Whitworth Wins Record 82d Event," *New York Times,* April 19, 1982, C9.

14. Ibid.

15. Associated Press, "Kathy Whitworth Wins 83d, a Record," *New York Times,* May 17, 1982, C8.

16. Kent Hannon, "Kathy Whitworth: Back on Her Game," *New York Times,* May 17, 1982, C8.

17. Elliott Kalb, *Who's Better, Who's Best in Golf* (New York: McGraw-Hill, 2006), 126.

18. Gordon S. White, Jr., "Wright, Whitworth Live Up to Legends," *New York Times,* April 28, 1985, S7.

19. "PGA Seniors Event Hangs Out the 'Men Only' Sign," *Chicago Tribune,* November 3, 1985, 10C.

20. Charles Bartlett, "6 Feet 11/2 Inches of Title Timber," *Chicago Daily Tribune,* August 9, 1958, A3.

21. Aaron Bracy, "Rankin Ready for Shot in Booth at ShopRite," *Courier-Post* (Cherry Hill, NJ), June 3, 2005, 2G.

22. Quoted in United Press International, "Caponi Gets Hall of Fame Nod," May 9, 2001.

CHAPTER 7. NANCY LOPEZ

1. Quoted in Gordon Edes, "Thanks to Nancy Lopez Ladies' Golf is Big Business," *Chicago Tribune,* July 8, 1979, K3.

2. Dave Anderson, "Nancy Lopez and Babe Zacharias," *New York Times,* July 13, 1979, A15.

3. Nancy Lopez with Peter Scwed. *The Education of a Women's Golfer* (New York: Simon & Schuster, 1979), 188.

4. Betty Cuniberti, "Lopez's Father Glimpsed Something Special Early," *Washington Post,* June 18, 1978, D1.

5. Grace Lichtenstein, "Burning Up the Links," *New York Times,* July 2, 1978, SM2.

6. Quoted in Betty Cuniberti, "Lopez's Father Glimpsed Something Special Early," *Washington Post,* June 18, 1978, D1.

7. Quoted in Gordon S. White, Jr., "Golf's Blazing Rookie Pro," *New York Times,* May 31, 1978, B11.

8. Quoted in Associated Press, "12-Year-Old Wins State Golf Title," *Los Angeles Times,* August 26, 1969, C1.

9. Lopez, *The Education of a Women's Golfer,* 23–24.

10. Quoted in "Morning Briefing," *Los Angeles Times,* August 23, 1971, E2.

11. Quoted in Lopez, *The Education of a Women's Golfer,* 24.

12. Quoted in Shav Glick, "Austin, Massey Toss It Away: Lopez Wins It," *Los Angeles Times,* March 13, 1978, D1.

13. Quoted in Cuniberti, "Lopez's Father Glimpsed Something Special Early."

14. Sally Jenkins, "Lopez Has Iron in Her Future," *Washington Post,* May 23, 1987, D1.

15. Quoted in John Radosta, "Miss Lopez, 20, Adds Spice to Golf Tourneys," *New York Times,* November 23, 1977, 26.

16. Jim Moriarty, "Thanks Nancy: Sharing Memories of Lopez' 25-Year Career," *Golf Digest,* October 2002, http://findarticles.com/p/articles/mi_moHFI/is_10_53/ai_93487313/print.

17. Quoted in Sheila Moran, "Lopez Wins—and Tears Flow," *Los Angeles Times,* January 27, 1978, F3.

18. Quoted in United Press International, "Nancy Lopez Wins First LPGA Title," *Los Angeles Times,* February 27, 1978, D3.

19. Quoted in Shav Glick, "Austin, Massey Toss It Away: Lopez Wins It," *Los Angeles Times,* March 13, 1978, D1.

20. Quoted in Associated Press, "Little Beats Lopez in Sudden Death," *Los Angeles Times,* March 20, 1978, D1.

21. Quoted in "Lopez Outlasts Idol Carner," *Chicago Tribune,* May 22, 1978, E5.

22. Quoted in "Lopez Captures Third Straight LPGA Tourney," *Chicago Tribune,* May 30, 1978, C4.

23. Quoted in "Lopez Grabs LPGA Title, Five Records," *Chicago Tribune,* June 12, 1978, E4.

24. Quoted in Betty Cuniberti, "Lopez Notches Fifth in Row, Tops $153,000," *Washington Post,* June 19, 1978, D1.

25. Ibid.

26. Quoted in Associated Press, "Nelson's 11 Is Aim for Lopez," *Washington Post,* June 20, 1978, D4.

27. Ibid.

28. Gregory Jaynes, "Miss Lopez's Streak Ends," *New York Times,* June 26, 1978, C9.

29. Ibid.

30. Quoted in Grace Lichtenstein, "Burning Up the Links," *New York Times,* July 2, 1978, SM2.

31. Arthur J. Morgan, "Mailbox: Nancy Lopez in Men's Tourneys Is Advocated," *New York Times,* July 2, 1978, S2.

32. "Morning Briefing: Psst! Don't Tell Jane Blalock Nancy Lopez Is Women's Golf," *Los Angeles Times,* July 11, 1978, G2.

33. Dave Anderson, "Beth Daniel: 'The Next Nancy Lopez,'" *New York Times,* July 22, 1978, 14.

34. "Lopez Wins Eighth, Sets Money Mark," *Washington Post,* August 7, 1978, D1.

35. John S. Radosta, "Miss Lopez on Star Course," *New York Times,* December 17, 1978, S5.

36. Gordon S. White, Jr., "L.P.G.A. Jealousy Is Denied," *New York Times,* May 6, 1979, 209.

37. Tribune Wire Services, "Old-Time Magic Casts Spell on All But Nancy Lopez," *Chicago Tribune,* May 21, 1979, D2.

38. Quoted in Edes, "Thanks to Nancy Lopez Ladies' Golf Is Big Business."

39. Dave Anderson, "Nancy Lopez and Babe Zacharias."

40. Associated Press, "Lopez-Melton Is a Winner Again," *Los Angeles Times,* March 22, 1982, D4.

41. Quoted in Gordon S. White, Jr., "A New Phase for Miss Lopez," *New York Times,* May 20, 1982, B19.

42. Nancy Lopez with Lisa D. Mickey, "The GFW Life: Nancy Hits the Road," *Golf for Women Magazine,* November–December 2002, http://www.golfdigest.com/gfw/gfwfeatures/index.ssf?/gfw/gfwfeatures/gfw200212lopez.html.

43. Quoted in Chicago Tribune Wires, "Lopez Wins LPGA by 8 Shots," *Chicago Tribune,* June 3, 1985, B4.

44. Ibid.

45. Quoted in Chicago Tribune wire, "Lopez Wins by 10 in Record Performance," *Chicago Tribune,* August 12, 1985, B2.

46. Lopez, "Nancy Hits the Road."

47. Quoted in Associated Press, "Lopez Wins to Qualify for Hall of Fame," *New York Times,* February 9, 1987, C5.

48. Gordon S. White, Jr., "Lopez Brings Home Third L.P.G.A. Title," *New York Times,* May 22, 1989, C9.

49. Clifton Brown, "Fans Let Lopez Know She Makes Their Cut," *New York Times,* July 6, 2002, D3.

50. Personal communication, Janet Coles, April 2007.

51. Quoted in Edes, "Thanks to Nancy Lopez Ladies' Golf Is Big Business."

52. Kalb, *Who's Better, Who's Best in Golf,* 221.

53. Eric Olson, Associated Press, "Nancy Lopez Takes Aim at LPGA, Wie," Honolulu Advertiser.com, March 7, 2007, http://the.honoluluadvertiser.com/article/2007/Mar/07/br/br8162370549.html?print=on.

Chapter 8. Other Great Players

1. Associated Press, "Joanne Carner Joins Women's Pro Golf Tour," *Washington Post,* October 21, 1969, D3.

2. United Press International, "Carner Really Turns Pro with Open Win," *Los Angeles Times,* June 28, 1971, C7.

3. Quoted in Gordon S. White, Jr., "Mrs. Carner Takes Open Golf Title," *New York Times,* July 13, 1976, 53.

4. Ibid.

5. Quoted in Rich Roberts, "Carner Has Been Cornering the LPGA Market," *Los Angeles Times,* March 27, 1980, E6.

6. Lopez, *The Education of a Women's Golfer,* 101–103.

7. Joe Cialini, "Little Hopeful for Golf Game," United Press International, June 24, 1991.

8. Personal communication, Janet Coles, April 2007.

9. Maureen Orcott, "Miss Stacy Beats Janet Aulisi By 1 Up to Keep Junior Crown," *New York Times,* August 16, 1970, 150.

10. Associated Press, "Stacy Wins 3d USGA Junior Girls Title," *Chicago Tribune,* August 15, 1971, B8.

11. World Golf Hall of Fame Profile: Pat Bradley, http://www.wgv.com/hof/member.php?member=1027.

12. Randall Mell, "U.S. Women's Open: It's All Inkster Annika Sorenstam Looks Unbeatable Again as the Final Round Begins, Then," *St. Paul Pioneer Press,* July 8, 2002, 1F.

13. World Golf Hall of Fame Profile: Ayako Okamoto, http://www.wgv.com/hof/member.php?member=1088.

14. LPGA Player Profile: Ayako Okamoto, http://www.lpga.com/content/2007PlayerBiosPDF/Okamoto-07.pdf.

15. Andrew Bagnato, "Alcott: Career a Success, Hall of Fame or Not," *Chicago Tribune,* August 25, 1992, 3C.

16. "Alcott, Daniel Qualify for LPGA Hall," *St. Louis Post Dispatch,* February 10, 1999, D1.

17. Joe Juliano, "Daniel Credits Lesson for First LPGA Victory," United Press International, July 18, 1983.

18. World Golf Hall of Fame Profile: Beth Daniel, http://www.wgv.com/hof/member.php?member=1044.

19. Peter Kessler, "Golftalk: Jan Stephenson," *Golf Magazine,* November 2003, http://www.golfonline.com/golfonline/features/kessler/columnist/0,17742,516199,00.html.

CHAPTER 9. THE LPGA SAILS UPWARD, GOES GLOBAL, AND
WITNESSES A GREAT RIVALRY

1. Personal communication, Janet Coles, April 2007.

2. Jaime Diaz, "L.P.G.A. Seeks Stability with Mechem," *New York Times,* February 3, 1991, S6.

3. Steve Brandon, "LPGA Seeks a Commissioner Who Can Do It All...and More," *The Oregonian,* September 7, 1990, E01.

4. Jim Burnett, *Tee Times: On the Road with the Ladies Professional Golf Tour* (New York: A Lisa Drew Book/Scribner, 1997), 130–131.

5. Personal communication, Charlie Mechem, April 2007.

6. Ibid.

7. Ibid.

8. Ibid.

9. Jaime Diaz, "Makeup Call; By Declaring War on CBS, Ben Wright Was Finally Able to Make Peace with Valerie Helmbreck," *Sports Illustrated,* May 18, 1998, G6.

10. Personal communication, Charlie Mechem, April 2007.

11. Ibid.

12. Ibid.

13. Ibid.

14. Peter Kessler, "Golftalk: Jan Stephenson," *Golf Magazine,* November 2003, http://www.golfonline.com/golfonline/features/kessler/columnist/0,17742,516199,00.html.

15. Personal communication, Pam Swensen, April 2007.

16. Charlie Nobles, "Webb and Sorenstam Ushering in a New Era," *New York Times,* January 12, 1997, S7.

17. Clifton Brown, "Sorenstam Should Test Herself," *New York Times,* March 3, 2003, D1.

18. Clifton Brown, "L.P.G.A.'s Best of 1997 Already Looking Forward to 1998," *New York Times,* December 16, 1997, C4.

19. Jack Cavanaugh, "Sorenstam Puts Her Mark in Big Apple Record Book," *New York Times,* July 20, 1998, C6.

20. Dave Allen, "Interview: Annika Sorenstam," *Golf Magazine,* August 2005, http://www.golfonline.com/golfonline/features/features/article/0,17742,1091814,00.html.

21. Michael Arkush, "Pak Wins, and Stops Sorenstam," *New York Times,* April 23, 2001, D6.

22. Clifton Brown, "Webb Wins as Sorenstam Sets Record," *New York Times,* November 19, 2001, D2.

23. Clifton Brown, "Improving on 2001, Sorenstam Wins 6th Tournament in 12 Starts," *New York Times,* July 1, 2002, D5.

24. Quoted in Jere Longman, "Female Athletes Gaining Ground and Breaking It," *New York Times,* February 25, 2003, D1.

25. Dave Anderson, "Sorenstam's Streak Stirs Mixed Ideas," *New York Times,* April 18, 2001, D1.

26. Susan K. Reed, "Annika, Honestly," *Golf for Women,* July/August 2006, http://www.golfforwomen.com/players/featured/2006/07/sorenstam_article_0706?currentPage=1.

27. Lena Williams, "Singh Can't Accept Sorenstam as a Foe," *New York Times,* May 13, 2003, D6.

28. Richard Sandomir, "Sorenstam vs. Men, Sorenstam vs. History," *New York Times,* May 16, 2003, D4.

29. Clifton Brown, "Sorenstam Misses the Cut After Scaling Her Everest," *New York Times,* May 24, 2003, D1.

30. Quoted in Jere Longman, "Female Athletes Gaining Ground and Breaking It."

31. Dennis Passa, "Sorenstam Wins, Sets Sights on Grand Slam," Associated Press Online, February 6, 2004.

32. Jonathan Okanes, "Sorenstam Is Quietly Dominating Tour Again," *Contra Costa Times,* October 6, 2005, F4.

33. Personal communication, Charlie Mechem, April 2007.

34. Jeff Shain, "Sorenstam Wins U.S. Women's Open," *Miami Herald,* July 3, 2006.

35. World Golf Hall of Fame Profile: Karrie Webb, http://www.wgv.com/hof/member.php?member=1121.

CHAPTER 10. THE PAK ATTACK AND THE FUTURE OF WOMEN'S GOLF

1. Eric Andelman, "Wie, Others Should Find a Role Model in Pak," ESPN the Magazine, June 15, 2006, http://sports.espn.go.com/golf/news/story?id=2480266.

2. Quoted in Paul Ramsdell, "Power Pak," *Rocky Mountain News,* September 20, 1998, 2C.

3. Mark Stewart, *Se Ri Pak: Driven to Win* (Brookfield, CT: The Millbrook Press, 2000), 6.

4. Ibid., 8.

5. Ibid., 9.

6. Ira Berkow, "Golf: Raised to Be a Champion; Father's Firm Push Sent Pak to the Top of Women's Golf," *New York Times,* July 28, 1998, C1.

7. Brad Townsend, "Tough Love: Se Ri Pak's Father Stands by His Unusual Training Methods," *Dallas Morning News,* August 3, 1998, 10B.

8. Ibid.

9. Berkow, "Golf: Raised to be a champion."

10. Patricia Davies, "Americans Hold on to Take World Amateur Team Title," *Times,* October 3, 1994.

11. Quoted in Clifton Brown, "Poised Pak Completes a Wire-to-Wire Victory," *New York Times,* May 18, 1998, C2.

12. Quoted in Jaime Diaz, "20/20; Unflappable Rookie Se Ri Pak and Easygoing Amateur Jenny Chuasiriporn, Both 20, Played 20 Extra Holes Before Pak Became the Youngest U.S. Women's Open champion," *Sports Illustrated,* July 13, 1998, 44.

13. Ben Dobbin, "Another Foreign-Born Phenom on Women's Golf Tour," Associated Press, May 27, 1998.

14. Jack Cavanaugh, "Sorenstam Aims to Push Pak Off Spotlight," *New York Times,* July 16, 1998, C4.

15. Liz Clarke, "LPGA's Tour De Force," *Washington Post,* July 14, 1998, E01.

16. Quoted in Stewart, *Se Ri Pak: Driven to Win,* 42.

17. "Se Ri Pak in LPGA Win," *Gold Coast Bulletin* (Australia), June 11, 2002, 32.

18. Associated Press, "Pak Wins LPGA Battle for the Ages," *Record* (Kitchener-Waterloo, Ontario), D4.

19. Dave Hackenburg, "Back in the Swing," *Toledo Blade,* July 9, 2006, T32.

20. Personal communication, author, April 2007.

21. Quoted in Jeffrey Reed, "Koreans Break Out of Pak," *London Free Press,* August 5, 2006, 18.

22. "Pak Receives 2006 Heather Farr Award," LPGA.com, http://www.lpga.com/content_1.aspx?pid=8654&mid=2.

23. Ibid.

24. Personal communication, Eric Fleming, April 2007.

25. Ron Kaspriske, "Korea in the News; On the Tee," *Golf Digest,* April 1, 2003, 65.

26. Ibid.

27. Personal communication, David H. Kim, April 2007.

28. Personal communication, Doris Kim, April 2007.

29. Ibid.

30. Ibid.

31. Personal communication, Eric Fleming, April 2007.

Chapter 11. Potential Great

1. Jennifer Mario, *Michelle Wie: The Making of a Champion* (New York: St. Martin's, 2006), 7.

2. Ibid., 8.

3. Ibid., 16.

4. Ibid., 29.

5. Ibid., 54.

6. Ibid., 101–3.

7. Ibid., 107.

8. "Wie Should Play Women: Campbell," *Calgary Herald,* May 18, 2002, F2.

9. Ian O'Connor, "Wie Hasn't Won, But Give Her Time," *Journal News* (Westerchester County, NY), July 18, 2006, 1C.

10. Daniel Pace, "Yang Makes Golf History Again," *Global News Wire*, October 10, 2006.

CHAPTER 12. THE INTRACTABLE COLOR LINE

1. Bruce Wright, *Black Robes, White Justice* (New York: A Lyle Stuart Book, 1987), 214.

2. Frederick Douglass, "The Color Line, The North American Review, June 1881," *The Life and Writings of Frederick Douglass* 4 (1955): 343–44 .

3. Andrew Hacker, *Two Nations: Black and White, Separate, Hostile, Unequal,* 2nd ed. (New York: Scribner, 1995), 3.

4. Cornel West, *Race Matters* (New York: Vintage Books, 1994).

5. Randall Kennedy, *Race, Crime and the Law* (New York: Random House, Inc., 1997), xii.

6. 163 U.S. 537 (1896).

7. *Brown v. Board of Education,* 347 U.S. 483, 495 (1954).

8. Jim Gullo, "Par for the Course," *American Legacy* 3 (1997): 37–41, 37.

9. *Evans v. Newton,* 382 U.S. 296, 299 (1966).

10. Clifton Brown, "In the Rough," *New York Times,* January 28, 2001, BR13.

11. Catherine M. Lewis, *"Don't Ask What I Shot": How Eisenhower's Love of Golf Helped Shape 1950s America* (New York: McGraw Hill, 2007), 95.

12. Red Smith, "Masters and Men," *New York Times,* March 23, 1973, 31.

13. Shirley Povich, "Mr. Brown Qualifies," *Washington Post,* February 3, 1970, D1.

14. George Dewan, "Black History Looking Back: He Battled an Uneven Lie; At golf's 1896 U.S. Open, a Black Teen's Race Was Misstated to Satisfy White Opponents," *Newsday,* January 16, 2007, H08.

15. Calvin H. Sinnette, "Golf's Ugly Legacy," *Baltimore Sun,* February 7, 1999, 1C.

16. Mark Maske, "Blue Says Women 1-Up on PGA," *Washington Post,* July 26, 1990, B4.

17. *Law v. Baltimore,* 78 F. Supp. 346, 349 (D. Md. 1948).

18. *Beal v. Holcombe,* 193 F.2d 384, 387 (5th Cir. 1951).

19. Alan Shipnuck, *The Battle for Augusta National: Hootie, Martha and the Masters of the Universe* (New York: Simon & Schuster, 2004), 25–26.

20. Jill Lieber, "Golf's Host Clubs Have Open-and-Shut Policies on Discrimination," *USA TODAY,* April 9, 2003, http://www.usatoday.com/sports/golf/2003-04-09-club-policies_x.htm.

21. Alison Lasseter, "Country Club Discrimination After Commonwealth v. Pendennis," *B.C. Third World Law Journal* 28 (2006): 311, 312 .

22. Bert Brechner, "Clubs Revisited," *Washington Post,* September 12, 1971, 269.

23. Colman McCarthy, "Snobbishness of the Masters Tournament," *Washington Post,* April 7, 1973, A18.

24. Molly Moore, "Loudoun Club Settles Discrimination Suit," *Washington Post,* January 12, 1984, B7.

25. "Blacks Accuse Oakland Golf Clubs of Bias," *Los Angeles Times*, September 16, 1985, 1.

26. "Black, Gifted and Snubbed," *Manchester Guardian Weekly*, June 22, 1997, 38.

27. Sinnette, "Golf's Ugly Legacy."

28. Ibid.

29. Shannon Rose, "Top 50 Most Influential Women of the Century," *Orlando Sentinel*, December 17, 1999, C6.

30. Quoted in Rhonda Glenn, "Pioneer Gregory Broke Color Barriers," USGA.com, February 2, 2005, http://www.usga.org/news/2005/february/gregory.html.

31. Quoted in Associated Press, "Althea Gibson Eyes Pro Golfing Career," *Washington Post*, June 24, 1961, C10.

32. "Althea Gibson Wins First Golf Tourney," *Chicago Defender*, July 22, 1961, 20.

33. "Tennis Star Althea Gibson Finds Golf Play a Stopper Instead of Romper, Beaten," *Chicago Defender*, August 29, 1962, 24.

34. "Althea Gibson on Verge of New Success in the World of Sports," *Chicago Defender*, July 27, 1963, 14.

35. Kahn, *The Lpga*, 125.

36. Ibid.

37. United Press International, "Althea Gibson's 68 Sets Course Mark," *New York Times*, August 6, 1966, 42.

38. Associated Press, "Mary Mills Gains Two-Stroke Lead," *New York Times*, August 7, 1966, 166.

39. Associated Press, "Althea Gibson Finds Golf Tough Game," *Washington Post*, June 18, 1967, D9.

40. Associated Press, "Ex-Tennis Queen Althea Gibson Planning Comeback at Age 41," *Los Angeles Times*, December 24, 1968, C3.

41. Ibid.

42. Personal communication, Dana Brooks, April 2007.

43. Rhonda Glenn, "Gibson's Athletic Prowess Took Her to Golf," February 8, 2006, http://www.usga.org/news/2006/february/gibson.html.

44. Candace Mayeron, "Renee Powell Survives Pressures to Make Good on Pro Golf Tour," *New York Times*, September 23, 1976, 67.

45. Elizabeth Wheeler, "Golf Is Just Cricket for Powell," *Los Angeles Times*, September 25, 1976, A1.

46. Associated Press, "Renee Powell Carries an Added Burden," May 15, 1974, *Los Angeles Times*, C11.

47. "Richmond Senior Women's Administrator Sugg Qualifies for 2006 U.S. Open," June 5, 2006, http://richmondspiders.cstv.com/genrel/060606aac.html.

48. "Player Rarity in LPGA History," *Richmond Times Dispatch*, August 7, 2000, C-1.

49. Gwen Daye Richardson, "A Big Thumbs Up to All Black Golfers," *USA TODAY*, July 21, 2000, 19A.

50. Personal communication, Dwight Lewis, April 2007.

51. "Attracting Black Golfers," *USA TODAY*, February 7, 1995, 1C.

52. Quoted in Rickey Hampton, "Woods' Impact Taking Foot in Flint Area," *Flint Journal,* August 14, 2006, C01.

53. Don Markus, "Greens Are Still Lacking Color; 10 Years After Woods Won at Augusta, Impact is Muted," *Baltimore Sun,* April 1, 2007, 1D.

54. Quoted in Vic Dorr Jr., "Conspicuously Absent," *Richmond Times Dispatch,* May 2, 2004, C-11.

Chapter 13. Gender Discrimination

1. Linda Lumsden, *Rampant Women: Women Suffragist and the Rights of Assembly* (Knoxville, TN: The University of Tennessee Press, 1997).

2. Ron Rapoport, *The Immortal Bobby: Bobby Jones and the Golden Age of Golf* (Danvers, MA: John Wiley & Sons, Co., 2005), 75.

3. Personal communication, Marsha Kazarosian, April 2007.

4. *Borne v. Haverhill Golf & Country Club, Inc.,* 791 N.E.2d 903, 908 (Mass. App. 2003).

5. *Borne,* 791 N.E.2d at 908–9.

6. Personal communication, Marsha Kazarosian, April 2007.

7. *Borne,* 791 N.E.2d at 914.

8. *Borne,* 791 N.E.2d. at 916.

9. Personal communication, Marsha Kazarosian, April 2007.

10. Eric Litchblau, "Woman Golfer Tees Off at Club's Policies," *Los Angeles Times,* February 17, 1989, at Metro, 2.

11. Ibid.

12. Engeler, "For Women Golfers, Life in the Rough," 42.

13. Alma Whitaker, "Midwick Bars Women Golf Players Who Seek Revenge," *Los Angeles Times,* April 7, 1916, III1.

14. Ibid.

15. Alan Shipnuck, *Battle for Augusta National.*

16. Ibid., 6.

17. Ibid., 9–10.

18. CNN Saturday, "Interview with Gloria Allred," Martha Zoller, September 28, 2002, Transcript # 092805CN.V27.

19. Doug Ferguson, AP, "LPGA wants Augusta Open to Women: 'Elitist' and 'Exclusionary,'" *National Post,* November 21, 2002, S4.

20. Ibid.

21. Eddie Pells, "LPGA Players to Augusta: 'Let the Women In,'" Associated Press, September 18, 2002.

22. Shipnuck, *Battle for Augusta National,* 328.

23. Quoted in John Husar, "The Locker Room," *Chicago Tribune,* June 30, 1968, B3.

24. Quoted in Miki Turner, "Challenging the Tradition Is the Norm," *Orange County Register,* July 30, 1995, CO8.

25. Personal communication, Susan Cayleff, April 2007.

26. Quoted in Ted Green, "Women in Sports: The Movement Is REAL," *Los Angeles Times,* April 23, 1974, B1.

27. Ibid.

28. Associated Press, "Man Wants to Join LPGA Tour," *Los Angeles Times,* November 1, 1973, D9; Gordon S. White Jr., "Commissioner Sees 'End of L.P.G.A.' If 2 Men Gain Entry to Tour," *New York Times,* July 27, 1979, A15.

29. 468 U.S. 609 (1984).

30. 481 U.S. 537 (1987).

31. 487 U.S. 1 (1988).

32. Nancy Kamp, "Gender Discrimination at Private Golf Clubs," *Sports Lawyer Journal* 5 (1998): 89, 101.

33. Scott R. Rosner, "Reflections on Augusta: Judicial, Legislative and Economic Approaches to Private Race and Gender Consciousness," *University of Michigan Journal of Law Reform* 37 (2003): 135.

34. H.R. 1817 (110th Congress).

35. H.Con. 7 (110th Congress).

36. "Its Springtime for the Men of Augusta National...But Still Winter for Women and Equality," April 3, 2007, http://maloney.house.gov/index.php?option=com_content&task=view&id=1314&Itemid=61.

37. Conn. Gen. Stat. § 52-571d(b) (2007).

38. Kamp, "Gender Discrimination at Private Golf Clubs," 105–6.

39. Personal communication, Pam Swensen, April 2007.

CHAPTER 14. THE FUTURE OF WOMEN'S GOLF

1. Randall Mell, "Golf Channel Breaks from Tradition with Tilghman," *South Florida Sun-Sentinel,* December 31, 2006.

2. Personal communication, Pam Swensen, April 2007.

3. Personal communication, Janet Coles, April 2007.

4. Personal communication, Charlie Mechem, April 2007.

5. Ibid.

6. Ibid.

7. Quoted in Bob Baptist, "2005 Honoree Betsy Rawls."

8. Nelson, "Mr. Golf Tees Off."

Selected Bibliography

Books

Burnett, Jim. *Tee Times: On the Road With the Ladies Professional Golf Tour.* New York: A Lisa Drew Book/Scribner, 1997.

Cayleff, Susan E. *Babe Didrikson: The Greatest All-Sport Athlete of All Time.* Berkeley, California: Conari Press, 1995.

Concannon, Dale. *Golf: The Early Days.* Vancouver, Canada: Cavendish Books, 1995.

Corcoran, Fred with Bud Harvey. *Unplayable Lies: The Story of Sport's Most Successful Impressario.* New York: Meredith Press, 1965.

Fraser, Antonia. *Mary Queen of Scots.* New York: Random House, 1969.

Frost, Mark. *The Grand Slam.* New York: Good Comma Ink, 2004.

Glenn, Rhonda. *The Illustrated History of Women's Golf.* Texas: Taylor Trade Publishing, 1991.

Guy, John. *The True Life of Mary Stuart: Queen of Scots.* New York: Houghton Mifflin Co., 2004.

Hasday, Judy L. *Extraordinary Women Athletes.* New York: Children's Press, 2000.

Lewis, Catherine M. *"Don't Ask What I Shot": How Eisenhower's Love of Golf Helped Shape 1950s America.* New York: McGraw Hill, 2007.

Lopez, Nancy with Peter Scwed. *The Education of a Women's Golfer.* New York: Simon & Schuster, 1979.

Lumsden, Linda. *Rampant Women: Women Suffragist and the Rights of Assembly.* Knoxville, TN: The University of Tennessee Press, 1997.

Mario, Jennifer. *Michelle Wie: The Making of a Champion.* New York: St. Martin's, 2006.

Nickerson, Elinor B. *Golf: A Women's History.* Jefferson, NC: McFarland & Company, Inc., 1987.

Rapoport, Ron. *The Immortal Bobby: Bobby Jones and the Golden Age of Golf.* Danvers, MA: John Wiley & Sons, Co., 2005.

Shipnuck, Alan. *The Battle for Augusta National: Hootie, Martha and the Masters of the Universe.* New York: Simon & Schuster, 2004.

Sommers, Robert. *Golf Anecdotes: From the Links of Scotland to Tiger Woods.* New York: Oxford University Press, 1995.

Stewart, Mark. *Se Ri Pak: Driven to Win.* Brookfield, CT: The Millbrook Press, 2000.

Tinkler, Basil Ashton. *Joyce Wethered: The Great Lady of Golf.* Stroud, Glouchester: Tempus Publishing Limited, 2004.

Weir, Allison. *Mary Queen of Scots and the Murder of Lord Darnley.* New York: Random House, 2003.

Wethered, Joyce. *Golfing Memories and Methods.* London: Hutchinson & Co., 1934.

Wright, Bruce. *Black Robes, White Justice.* New York: A Lyle Stuart Book, 1987, 214.

Newspapers and Magazines

Associated Press
Chicago Defender
Chicago Tribune
Golf Digest
Golf for Women Magazine
Los Angeles Times
New York Times

Web Sites

Executive Women's Golf Foundation
    http://www.ewga.com/
The First Tee
    http://www.thefirsttee.org/custom/intro.html
Ladies Golf Union
    http://www.lgu.org/
LPGA
    http://www.lpga.com
National Golf Foundation
    http://www.ngf.org/cgi/home.asp
Professional Golf Teachers Association
    http://www.pgtaa.com/
United States Golf Association
    http://www.ewga.com/
World Golf Hall of Fame
    http://www.wgv.com/hof/member.php?member=1085

Index

ABOUT THE AUTHOR

DAVID L. HUDSON, JR., is the author or coauthor of fifteen books, among them *Boxing's Most Wanted* (2003) and *Basketball Championships' Most Wanted: The Top 10 Book of March Mayhem, Playoff Performances, and Tournament Oddities* (2006). He is Research Attorney at the Freedom Forum First Amendment Center at Vanderbilt University and Adjunct Instructor at Middle Tennessee State University.